MW00475010

Withdrawn

I Did a New Thing

ALSO BY TABITHA BROWN

Seen, Loved and Heard

Cooking from the Spirit

Feeding the Soul (Because It's My Business)

4024261
ITEM # 15464307

158.1
BRO

110916/4

I Did a New Thing

30 Days to Living Free

TABITHA BROWN

wm

WILLIAM MORROW
An Imprint of HarperCollins*Publishers*

Edwardsville Public Library
112 South Kansas Street
Edwardsville, IL 62025

I DID A NEW THING. Copyright © 2024 by Tabitha Brown.
All rights reserved. Printed in the United States of America.
No part of this book may be used or reproduced in any
manner whatsoever without written permission except in
the case of brief quotations embodied in critical articles
and reviews. For information, address HarperCollins
Publishers, 195 Broadway, New York, NY 10007.

HarperCollins books may be purchased for educational,
business, or sales promotional use. For information,
please email the Special Markets Department at
SPsales@harpercollins.com.

FIRST EDITION

Designed by Bonni Leon-Berman

Library of Congress Cataloging-in-Publication Data has
been applied for.

ISBN 978-0-06-328611-5

23 24 25 26 27 LBC 5 4 3 2 1

This one is for me. For Tab.

Contents

Contents

Contents

Y'all Alright?

Hello there!

Years ago, I did a personal challenge that I called "I Did a New Thing!" Every single time I did the challenge, I would learn something different about myself and my mind would expand. There's something about stepping outside of your comfort zone, right? When you do things you've never done before, yes, it can be scary—but it can also be freeing. And y'all know Tab is all about living free, yes?

The challenge was really simple. For thirty days I would do something I'd never done before. It didn't matter if it was big or small—the only requirement was that I challenged myself to think outside of what I would consider my "normal." The only rule was that I did something new. Sometimes it was something simple, like trying a different food or buying and wearing a different color lipstick. Other times, I'd step it up a bit and go somewhere I never went before or speak to someone I'd never spoken to before. Still other times, I'd do the hard thing—have that tough conversation with a friend or set my fears aside and push my mind, body, and spirit further than I'd ever gone before. Here are a few posts from my earliest challenge in 2014:

My baby girl and #IDidaNewThing. We did a wine hydrating mask together! I didn't think it did anything different until we washed it off! Wow! Our faces felt like silk. This moment not only left my skin feeling amazing; it brought my daughter and me so much laughter and closeness—something that's needed in those teenage years. I'm so grateful! Will definitely add this to my favorite things.

So tonight #IDidaNewThing. I had date night with my son! As soon as I sat down on the floor, he said "Mommy you have a good day?" I said, "Yes my dude, thank you for asking" and before I could ask him, he said "Love you Mommy." Wow! He never ceases to AMAZE me. He fed me and we talked about Thomas the Train and pumpkin patches. Lol. Every day he teaches me more patience. I'm learning to create more little moments so that one day they become big memories. Our children are only children for such a small amount of time, and we must enjoy it while we can.

#IDidaNewThing I wasn't sure I would be able to handle this screening tonight of #TheTheoryofEverything but #EddieRedmayne was so honest and true in his role of Stephen Hawking that it made it so worth it! This movie was so simply amazing! #ALS

That last one was really a life-changing new thing. I'd cried so much that night before attending the screening because I knew it was going to trigger my emotions about losing my mother to ALS.

I almost didn't go. But I pushed through and there was an emotional blessing on the other side of it. Although it caused so much emotion, the movie was so therapeutic for me. It made me see how strong I was. It also brought me comfort knowing this movie would bring more awareness to ALS. That's the power of this challenge. Every single time I've done it over the years, I've seen how taking a leap of faith allows God to open up a new lane for me.

In 2017, one of the "new things" I tried was a thirty-day vegan challenge. And listen, God showed *up,* honey! I'd been struggling with illness for nearly a year and was desperately searching for healing and just desired to feel normal again! Remember that old saying? "Doing the same thing over and over again and expecting different results is the definition of insanity." Well, Tab wasn't going crazy no more, okay? I challenged myself to eat vegan every day for thirty days, yes, to improve my health, but also to better my life. Can I tell you just how those thirty days changed my entire life? It took me on a journey where I was able to heal myself of the sickness that was attacking my body and create a new mindset of freedom. Here we are, six years later, and my life has never been the same. All because I decided to do a new thing. I am so grateful I gave myself thirty days to try to improve my health. It did that and more!

And guess what, honey? Change can happen for you, too. When I was thinking about writing another book, I kept coming back to that point in my life when everything felt broken and out of reach. I kept remembering what it took for me to live outside of what everything and everyone wanted me to be—from my hair to my voice to my work. It took me deciding that every day I would do something I'd never done before. I set my mind and heart on something new and let God do the rest.

Now, maybe your "new things" aren't the same as mine. That's 100 percent okay. The messages that God has given me will still apply whether you are going on some grand vacation or simply deciding to apply for the promotion. Because here's the truth: Your freedom and transformation aren't about how big or small that new thing is. It's about what God is saying to us all through them. My whole life is a testimony to what can happen when you release the noise, comparisons, and outside perceptions and simply do the new thing. And I want that so much for you!

So let's try it for thirty days! No, it's not exactly like the vegan challenge where we did one new thing for thirty days. This time, we will do one new thing *every single day,* for the next thirty days. And honey, you don't have to wait until Monday or the beginning of a new month or year to get started. There's no set time and place or any extra preparation required. All you have to do is show up for yourself. And that can start right now.

As you move through the book, I will share with you some of my most recent "new things" and all I've learned from them. But honey, I'm not the only one out here doing new things! Many of you are already on that journey. I want to thank Tracey Michae'l Lewis-Giggetts for taking the time to gather stories from some of my play cousins—that's what I call all of you who support and follow me—out there. Doing a new thing has changed so many people's lives that, with her help, I decided to include several of those stories throughout these pages so you'll know you're not alone. In every chapter, I will offer you a prompt that will hopefully give you some direction in figuring out your "new thing," as well as some potential options for new things you might do that day. But honey, please don't feel like you *have* to do what I suggest. If I say "do something fun" but you decide to "do something courageous," that's your business and alright with me.

Remember, the only rule is to do a new thing. This challenge is about you walking on your own freedom journey, whatever that might look like for you. Listen, if you want to try more than one thing in a day, you can do that, too, because again, that's your business. The goal here is simply to open our minds and hearts, to face our fears and insecurities, and find a new love for ourselves. During this process you'll also come to understand what you don't like, and honey, that's a very good thing! Sometimes we do a new thing just to learn that we will never do that thing again, alright?

The purpose in taking this journey with me is for you to spend this next month discovering new things about yourself and new things about the world. It doesn't matter where you are from, where you are financially, what you have or don't have—we all can do something new every day and open a new part of ourselves. The beautiful thing is, we will do it together!

So let's go on and get into it, shall we?

Do Something Fearless

> "Too many of us are not living our dreams
> because we are living our fears."
> —Les Brown

I did a new thing today.

It's my mama's birthday, and while she's been gone for fifteen years now, there are days that she feels so, so close. Days when I know she's watching me with so much pride from her place in Heaven. Today is no exception.

I flew to San Francisco to be a keynote speaker for the company Salesforce. The theme of the program was "Representation Matters," and it was my first time speaking there. Now listen, I'm not unfamiliar with doing these kinds of events at all. I've been speaking quite a bit over the last few years. But for some reason, honey, today felt different. The spirit of my mama had been so very present all day long. From the time I woke up, she'd been heavy on my heart and mind, and this is her spirit's normal, especially on her birthday! Sometimes she comes with a message or a clear sign to let me know she is very much present. I never expect to know what the sign will be—I just allow it to unfold!

And it did. When we first got to town, we went to breakfast. While sitting there waiting for our food, the song "Fix You" by Coldplay played through the restaurant's speakers. Honey, when I tell you the tears just flowed. I was so overwhelmed as memories flooded my mind and heart. If you read my first book, you might remember me sharing how my mom leaves me dimes as a sign that she's with me. It's something she told me she'd do before she passed away. So now, whenever I see dimes, I know that's a hug and a kiss from my mama. Well, in 2014, my sister and I decided to do a short film about the dimes with my sister playing my mother in it. We used "Fix You" on the soundtrack of the film. With my mama being so heavy on my heart that whole morning, hearing the song sent me to a deeply emotional place. Honey, I lost it right there. Tab was no more good.

My first thought was *I know this is my mama just giving me a sign that she is present and she's around me.* But I didn't know just how true that would be until later that day when, right before I stepped on the stage to speak, one of my assistants said, "Oh my God, Tab! Look on top of that production case!" When I looked over, what do you think I saw? Yep, there was a dime. Moma was saying, "Girl, I am here on my birthday to watch my baby." Curious, I picked up the dime because I usually always check the year. Sure enough, it was 2014. The same year we did the film about her and used the song we heard earlier.

Talk about mind-blowing! Honey, Moma was just getting started though. After I spoke, there was a meet and greet and I met a man who told me his wife was a huge fan.

"Oh my goodness," I said. "Well give me your phone and let me do a video to say hello to her. What's her name?"

He said, "Patricia . . . or Pat."

I wish you all could have seen my face. Patricia is my mama's name. She was just showing all the way out, ya hear?

Needless to say, my heart was filled with so much gratitude. After the meet-and-greet portion of the program, I was asked if I wanted to go to the top floor of the Salesforce building as it is the tallest building west of the Mississippi. Now this is where I did my new thing, honey. Because Tab don't really play with heights like that. I love hiking but even then, I've learned that if we get too high up on the mountain, I get nervous. And I suppose I could have let my fear lead me. I could have said no and chosen to stay on the lower floors. But Moma had been pushing me all day to be present in every single moment. To know that she was with me no matter what I did or where I went. So with "Fix You" playing as a soundtrack in my heart and holding on to my determination to do something I ordinarily wouldn't do, I got in the elevator and watched as we climbed seemingly into the sky. And my God, my God. The city was so glorious and beautiful from that vantage point. It looked like we were in another country. I could see for miles and miles including all of San Francisco, all of Oakland, the Golden Gate Bridge, the Oakland Bridge, and even Alcatraz. I was able to see from my bird's-eye view all these different places that hold so much history. And that's when it hit me. The lesson I was supposed to take from choosing to do my new thing:

There's so much more to see when we are willing to climb a little bit higher. When we are willing to push ourselves just a little bit further. Yes, we might be afraid. You might even be shaking in your boots, honey. But guess what? When we embrace the moment and choose to "do it afraid" (whatever *it* might be for you), we get to see things we've never seen before. God gets to show us something He couldn't show us before because we didn't have the courage to put ourselves at a higher vantage point. What if I'd said, "No, I can't go up there. It's just too high and I don't want to see all that." Honey, I would've missed out on all that breathtaking beauty; the magnitude of that area's rich history would have been lost to me.

Being up that high also made me feel like I was closer to Moma. I get that same feeling on planes sometimes, too. As I look out the window and see the clouds, I feel like I'm touching a little bit of Heaven. So when I found myself at the top of the Salesforce building, I couldn't help but think, *Wow, this is a different view. If I'm seeing all this beauty, I wonder what Moma sees.* In fact, I often wonder what all the ones who sit high and look low—our angels, our ancestors, God—must see. I am so thankful that I get even a small glimpse of that for myself.

If I'm honest, I've always been a fearless spirit. I've always been of the mindset that if we don't try, we won't know. I remember growing up and my parents having some fears about doing anything that required us to go beyond our city. They were traditional in that way and often couldn't see themselves doing more than what they were doing. I understand now that they were being protective. We didn't have a lot of money growing up, and their first priority was making sure we had all that we needed. But I think the result of that was, honey, Tab wanted to see everything!

The thing I'm most grateful for is they always pushed me toward my dreams. My mama may have had her fears and doubts about what she could do, but she always encouraged me to go after the things I wanted. "Go on and do your acting thing, baby. Go 'head and get into fashion," she'd say. Both my parents believed that I could do more than them and they planted the seed of that fearlessness in me.

That's why in these instances when I may have some anxiety about doing something, I listen to that pressing of my mama's spirit. I can hear her say "You go on now." And that just drains that fear right on out of me. I know now what it means to be truly free, and part of that freedom is making sure that I don't walk in fear. I can't love myself and be fearful all the time. Loving ourselves gives us the courage to do exactly what you're doing right now— new things. Being fearless is how we're supposed to live, I truly believe that.

Today I learned just a little bit more about what it means to be truly free. It doesn't mean that we won't ever be afraid. We are human and have every right and ability to feel the full range of emotions available to us. It also doesn't mean we won't have some hesitation about pushing ourselves above and beyond our comfort zones. Even someone like me, who tries to live as free as possible every day, might need a little push from Heaven, like my mama did for me. But freedom does mean that we challenge ourselves to set our fears aside and trust ourselves enough to choose courage and experience something amazing. Freedom means being willing to stretch in order to become our best selves.

So here's to day one, honey. Go to the top of the mountain. Take your fear with you. But don't ever let it stop you from seeing new things and reaching new heights. There's a big world out there, and it's waiting for all of us—I know that for sure.

TSA
(Tabitha Service Announcement)

We can give fear two different types of power:
the positive kind or the negative.
Let's fuel it wisely!

From Tab's "New Thing" Catalog

Try hiking for the first time. So many people are worried about bugs and hills and animals, but don't forget there's also fresh air, healthy movement, and the beauty of nature and community.

Take a ride on an escalator. *What, Tab?!* Yes, honey. My granny was so afraid of escalators, and I know many people who don't fool with them. Thank God that when she did a new thing and finally got on one, she realized it "wasn't that bad." Now that's a word! You just might find out that the thing you are avoiding because you're scared is not as scary as you thought.

Learn to ride a bike. This is another one that some might question. But listen, my mama was afraid of riding bikes. Apparently when she was a little girl, she had a terrible fall and never got back on. Are you afraid of something because of one event that happened long ago? Honey, that was then and this is now. Ain't nothing wrong with trying again.

Do Something That Taps Your Inner Child

"The most sophisticated people I know—
inside they are all children."
—Jim Henson

I did a new thing today.

I went to the Emmys!

You might be saying, "Yass, Tab! Good for you!" But let me just tell you what this day has meant for me and why I feel compelled to share this particular new thing with you here. In addition to being nominated for an Emmy for my children's show *Tab Time*, I also presented three awards in person. And I must say, honey, there was something powerful about standing on the Wilshire Ebell Theatre stage and holding that trophy alongside some of the greatest actors, storytellers, and creators alive today. Even getting my credentials and having people stop and congratulate me as I went to rehearsals gave me such a charge in my body. Everything felt surreal as I thought about the twenty years before. All the auditions. All the things I did to my body and mind to change myself into something I wasn't, only to find success being exactly and always myself. Going to the Emmys is a dream that I've shared with my husband for the last twenty-plus years of our lives, and tonight I heard him say to me what he's always said: "It's going to be me and you tonight, babe! We are going up in there and we are going to be clean. We are going to be sharp, okay?!" And we were! Both of our hearts were overflowing with joy. There was one point in the night when we just looked at each other and almost at the same time said, "We already won, babe. We've been winning for so long together. God has blessed us in such a way that just being here is the win." It was and is truly a journey of a lifetime. All I can say is "Ooh God, I thank you!"

But in all the hustle and bustle of preparing for the Emmy ceremonies, the thing I was most excited about was my dress. Now listen, many people know that one of the first questions an actor is asked when they hit any Hollywood red carpet is "Who are you wearing?" Well, I was so overjoyed to tell the world that my dress was made by a seven-year-old fashion designer from Edison, New Jersey, named Brooke Lauren. Yep, read that again. The *designer* of that gorgeous orange and pink tulle dress is *seven*, honey. And *that* was totally a new thing for me also. See, I've worked with many designers over the last few years and have had the good fortune of wearing some amazing pieces. However, to venture out and have a child design my gown was new and wonderful in every way. And when I say she nailed it, this sweet baby *really* nailed it. The dress makes me so happy and fits my personality perfectly.

It gives me so much joy to create space for other people to shine. I'm so grateful for this platform to elevate others. Working with Brooke Lauren was intentional on my part. It was important for me to be at this special Emmys ceremony for children's television and programming and have a child design my dress. I wanted her to be elevated, not just to the world, but within herself. I wanted her to know what it's like to dream, and to see her dreams already come to pass even before she really understands how big a platform she's on. I may not have brought home the Emmy, but I definitely brought home the win because the joy I felt, the love I felt, especially in knowing that I was able to bless this sweet little girl, *that* was everything!

I met Ms. Brooke for the first time during the dress fitting and it did my soul good to be able to witness the wonderful imagination of this seven-year-old child's mind—so innocent and pure of heart. When I walked in to meet Brooke, she was so cool and calm in her shiny gold dress and shiny gold sneakers. I thought, *Wow, she is like a little lady.* We talked about how she was feeling being in California for the first time and the awards show experience. She was excited and happy but still very calm. But honey, the moment I tried on the dress and walked out for her to see me, her eyes got big and her mouth was wide open! She said, "You look beautiful! Just like I imagined!" Baby, that almost took me out! She was so proud of herself, and it made me so grateful at that moment. That was also when I figured out what God was trying to say to me through this new thing I was doing.

The more we are able to tap into the child within us, the more we'll find our purest form of thinking and living. Children are the best demonstrators of freedom we have. They move and create with such wild abandon. Because of that, there's so much value in giving our inner children voice and space to be what we might not have been able to be way back when. For me, Little Tab longed for the freedom to be. So it makes sense that so much of what I do, so much of what I talk about, is being and staying free. And honey, there have been times when I've forgotten. For a long time, I used to wear high heels because I thought this is how a woman is supposed to be. High heels automatically mean sexy. But when I began to tap into my inner child and her mission to be free, I realized that I felt most like myself, most free, in sneakers. I was what they called a tomboy back in the day and spent most of my time running around and climbing trees. So grown Tab put them heels away, honey. And now, I can have on a designer, couture gown and honey, I'm gonna be just as sexy as I would be in some high heels, but I'm also going to be comfortable and present!

That's truly the benefit I've experienced from tapping into my inner child. I get to tend to her in a way that maybe I couldn't before. And as a result, I can feel her pleasure. I get to tell her, "Remember when you watched Keshia Knight Pulliam as Rudy on *The Cosby Show* and you longed to be an actress like her? Well, look at us now, baby girl. We did it!" The great thing about Little Tab is she was always patient. She was always waiting. Honey, your inner child is patiently waiting for you to get to where they believe you can go. The child in us is always free. It's the adult in us who gets tainted by the world. We are taught that we're not enough, or we embrace our fear and doubt. But talking to our younger selves can help us remember who we really are.

On my tough days, I hold on to what Little Tab knows. My mama used to always tell me, "Give grace to people. Love people. Try to find the good in everybody." And despite how hard that is—the fact that Adult Tab knows how hard it is to trust people, the more successful she gets—I try to tap into that lesson.

So let's think more like a child. When you are afraid, think more like a child and take the leap anyway, trusting that someone, if only God, will catch you if you fall. When you want to celebrate, think more like a child. Dance like no one—or everyone—is watching, whichever gets you moving. When you're trying to create business, access your childlike imagination that says that not even the sky's the limit. Put your planner and phone down for a pair of seconds and get into the playfulness and joy of living. Children are so free until, of course, the world tells them they're not. Until adults pile on and project their pain onto them. But even then, children have a marvelous kind of resilience. What would your life look like if you could tap into the wonder of your inner child and approach your life and dreams in such a liberating way? I suspect it would be *very good*.

TSA
(Tabitha Service Announcement)

As a child we are all free, until we are taught
otherwise. Tap back into that freedom, honey!

From Tab's "New Thing" Catalog

Try wearing a color that you never wear. If you love to wear black, try a bright color or pattern. If you are normally in bright colors like me, maybe try wearing black.

Try a new drink. My brother Nic just finished a cleanse and, honey, he has fallen in love with beet juice. You never know if you'll like something if you don't try it!

Take a different route home. My daddy always taught me to never go the same way home every day so that people don't learn your route. That's great for safety, but you can also do it to change your scenery, which is helpful in soothing your mind.

Meet My Play Cousin...
Chandra Did a New Thing

When I was little, maybe around five or six years old, my mother would take me to the playground and I would make a beeline straight to the slides. It was my favorite thing to do. It didn't matter how big the slide was to my barely three-foot-tall self, I'd climb to the top of that ladder, swing my legs around, put my hands in the air, and slide to the very end. Sometimes it was a straight slide. You know, the metal kind that burned your legs in the summertime. Sometimes it was the twisty, spiral plastic slide that I'd get stuck in because the material used on the slide would not allow me to move any further once I got halfway down. Then I'd have to scoot all the way to the end. I loved sliding as a kid, but of course, as I became a teenager and started hanging out with friends at the mall, all those fun things we used to do as children went away.

When I had my son, Shawn, I knew that the first thing I would do when he got old enough was to take him to the playground and introduce him to my favorite thing—the slide. When he was nothing but a little thing, I encouraged him to walk up the ladder, and every single time he went to the top, he would sit there and just cry his little eyes out. My son hated the slide. Devastating! But he totally loved the swings. Swinging was his thing, to the point that if I put him on the swing, he would not get off the entire time we were there. As I pushed my baby and he giggled and laughed as his little legs and feet moved back and forth like I taught him, I couldn't help but glance longingly over at the slide, remembering a time when joy just seemed to come so easy.

Then one day I was out with one of my mom friends and we decided to take both of our children out to this new park nearby. Right there, in the middle of the playground, was a beautiful piece of art... wait, I mean... a huge, wide metal slide. Thankfully it was fall and not summertime, so it wasn't burning hot. I rubbed my hand up and down the slide, knowing full well that my baby boy wasn't going anywhere near it.

In the name of small talk, I shared the story of how I used to love to slide when I was a kid with my friend, and she said, "Go do it!"

"What? What do you mean? Do what?"

"Get on the slide," she said.

"At this big age, you want me to get up on that ladder and slide down. At this park. With all these kids and parents looking at me?"

"Yes, that's absolutely what I want you to do."

I just stared at her.

We continued walking around the park. I pretended that the conversation didn't happen and pushed my son on the swings for what seemed like forever. She took her daughter to the seesaw and used her hand to push the other side. Looks like her baby girl found her favorite thing, too. Still, I couldn't help but keep thinking about what she asked me to do.

There was a part of me, maybe that little kid inside, that also was saying, "Do it. Why not? Who cares what people think?" And I know she was right. Surely the children weren't concerned about it. They probably would just find it funny that a grown-up was on the slide. They actually might join me. And the parents? Well, they were going to think whatever they want to think.

You know what? This is an opportunity for me to do something that I haven't done in decades. So, why not?

"I'm going to do it," I said, mostly to myself but to my friend also.

"Great."

She took my baby boy's hand. I smiled at him and gave him a big kiss on the cheek. "Mommy's going to go on the slide," I said. He shrugged and said, "Okay." Apparently, it wasn't a big deal to him.

I climbed to the top of the ladder, which seemed way narrower than I remembered. I was afraid I was going to break the whole thing, because again: an adult on a slide. But realizing that it was made of steel and bolted to the ground, I figured I was pretty safe. When I got to the top, it dawned on me that it was a very different view up there when you're in your thirties as opposed to a kindergartner. It certainly didn't look as big or intimidating as it may have looked to me as a child. But something still shifted in me when I instinctually put my hands in the air and released my body down the slide.

It was like a powder keg of joy just exploded in my chest. And when I made it to the bottom of the slide, I looked up at my friend and she was just smiling so hard. I was smiling back at her when I heard it. The sudden sound of—applause? There were at least five moms and two dads who were giving me a full ovation. And it was the funniest, most exhilarating thing I've ever experienced. My new thing changed me that day. I gave my inner child a voice, and I will always be glad that I did.

Do Something That Celebrates You

"You are a firecracker in everything you do.
Celebrate yourself every day."
—Hiral Nagda

I did a new thing.

I threw myself a party, honey! It was important for me to take time out to celebrate my Emmy nomination with all my family and friends, and let me tell you, it was some of the best fun I've had in a long time. The party was held at the Pendry Hotel, in their private club called the Britely. The room I reserved downstairs was very retro and colorful, with splashes of pink, green, yellow, orange, red, and blue—just like my show. The space also has a bowling alley, which was great because I wanted my party to also have something the kids could do. It was a sneaker ball, so while everyone dressed up in their finest, I wanted that fun element, too. We decked the space out in the *Tab Time* theme colors and had cutouts, step-and-repeats, and fresh flowers. Again, pretty much everything that embodied the show. Of course there was plenty of vegan food and we made fun green drinks like an "Avi Juice," named after the animated avocado from the show. Honey, I had on my avocado blinged-out sneakers, and we all partied like we never partied before.

It was so much fun and there was so much joy in the room, despite the fact that I ultimately didn't win the award. But you know what was the biggest response to all the photos and videos I posted about the party? Nearly everyone I talked to said some version of "Thank you, Tab, for celebrating yourself. Being nominated is just as worthy of celebration as a win. Thank you for teaching me to celebrate myself at every stage of the journey."

Listen, God wasted no time getting me the message today, you hear?

So many people will find out they are up for a promotion, then not get the promotion and think they don't have the right to celebrate themselves. Baby, you were still considered, right? Isn't it wonderful that your skills and work ethic meant that you were in the running? There are others who don't celebrate the fact that they get to *try* to have a baby, even if it hasn't happened for them yet. And honey, Tab knows. Simply talking about all it takes to try to conceive can be triggering for some of us. So many are dealing with a lot of grief around fertility issues and losses, so it can get really hard to even try to be positive. Our emotions can be all over the place and, out of fear, we choose not to talk about it—much less celebrate our efforts—because we think we will jinx ourselves or something. But honey, I'm of the mind that we should always celebrate the process. We should pause a minute to take in just how far we've come and where we are on this journey called life— even if we haven't reached the destination we want.

Too many people are focused on the win and not enough of us are giving ourselves credit for the work it took to get where we are. The "trying" of a thing matters, too, honey. You get to celebrate the fact that you are trying to bring forth life, no matter the outcome. You get to celebrate the fact that you are brave enough to do it, sometimes over and over again. You get to celebrate that you are strong enough to say "Let's give it another go." And if you decide to not give it another go, that's also bravery and it should be acknowledged that you made the best decision for yourself. That's a win all by itself.

Sure, everyone celebrates themselves differently. Maybe a party is not your thing. But whatever it is, I think we must be intentional about setting aside time to really celebrate ourselves. That's something I know I'm really trying to get better at myself. I tend to just put my head down and work. I stay so focused on this work I'm called to do that sometimes I don't stop and celebrate. But if there is one thing I've learned, it's that if you don't celebrate you, nobody else will. They'll think, "Oh, well, if she ain't celebrating it, then it must not be a big deal." So sometimes your celebration of yourself is so other people know that you want and like to be celebrated.

And as I said, self-celebration looks different from person to person. I like a spa day or to change my hair, but it might be different for you. Celebrating yourself might actually mean stepping away from the very thing you're celebrating. For me, that looks like a whole vacation, honey. Tab needs a break sometimes, y'all. It allows me to be able to truly breathe and recharge a bit. Don't be afraid to step away from the very thing that you're celebrating yourself for. We all need to periodically step back and look at this thing we do and make sure that we are still doing it the way we feel like we should be doing it. Whatever celebrating yourself looks like, the biggest gift you can give yourself is simply acknowledging that you did it. You are not an imposter. You do deserve it. Get in that mirror and tell yourself "I did that." Be excited about your efforts. Be excited about your achievements and celebrate accordingly.

Honey, you are worthy of celebration just because. You might not be going to the Emmys or have been nominated for an award. Your life might be and look totally different from mine, and that's okay. Because as I've said, you don't necessarily need to have won a single thing to celebrate yourself. Maybe just getting up this morning is reason enough to treat yourself. Maybe the fact that every day you try to do and be better is enough for you to throw yourself a party with the people who love and support you. Celebrate yourself, and if anyone questions you about it, tell them Tab said you can do it if you want to because that's your business.

TSA
(Tabitha Service Announcement)

Being alive is worthy of a celebration!
You're still here.

From Tab's "New Thing" Catalog

Write a love letter to yourself. Honey, share with yourself everything about you that you love from the physical to the emotional to the spiritual.

Take yourself on a day date to a museum or an art gallery. When you arrive, take some time to see what the art says to you personally. Sometimes when we look at art, we can find something to celebrate about ourselves, or we can see ourselves in the art.

Take yourself to the park for a solo picnic. Baby, set your little blanket out, have a fun little basket with your favorite treats, bring along your favorite book or journal, and allow the wind to hit your face. It'll be a beautiful thing.

DAY 4

Do Something New ... but Check Your Triggers

"You may not control all the events
that happen to you, but you can decide
not to be reduced by them."
–Maya Angelou

I did a new thing.

I had a second, more extensive mammogram and ultrasound on my breasts.

Now, y'all know Tab believes in living and being healthy. In addition to eating vegan and working out regularly, I try to make sure I get to all my preventative care appointments. Since I turned forty, those appointments now include regular mammograms. I'd missed my first one because it was scheduled at the beginning of the pandemic when everything shut down. But I'd finally gotten my first appointment, and now I was back for a follow-up.

I initially didn't think too much of the doctor asking me to get another mammogram, one that uses a different—and way more intense—cup to compress the breast. I just figured that like many women, my breasts had what is often called "high density," and this was a precaution. But it was more than that. After they did the mammogram, the doctor said there was something seen on the film that was of concern, and asked me to move to the ultrasound room so they could get a better look.

"Ms. Brown, we still see what appears to be a small mass in your right breast. It could be absolutely nothing or it could be something, but because it's your first mammogram, we don't know how long it's been there. It's probably nothing, but we want to be sure."

Thankfully, my husband was there with me in the lobby, and they allowed him to come in as the next step was explained.

"We'll have to do a biopsy."

Now, honey, I would be lying to you if I said this didn't make me a little bit flustered and nervous. It did. And maybe there was a part of me deep down that wanted to freak out a little bit. I remember just sitting there. Taking deep breaths. For a minute, everything felt numb. Then I went to the mirror: *No, ma'am. Don't you go there.*

I *could* have, in this new moment with this new news and doing this new thing of getting a compression mammogram and ultrasound on my breast, lost my mind. I *could* choose to get on the internet and start to look up a ton of different people's horror stories about what that mass could be and stress myself out. I *could* choose to start telling myself that it's something before I even knew if that was true. But I'm not doing any of that. I'm choosing to allow it to just be. I'm choosing to say, "Okay, they found something. It could be nothing. It could be something, but I won't know until I get the biopsy. So there's no need for me to start stressing about it now."

Even later, as I was preparing for the breast biopsy, I had to wrestle with them triggers as they kept trying to rear their heads. Yes, I woke up knowing that I was going to do something that I never, ever desired to do, that I never thought I would have to do. No one wakes up and automatically thinks, "Oh, there'll be a lump in my breasts." No one wants to have a compression mammogram and a biopsy. No one wants to be afraid. But those days come. Those days happen. And when they do, sometimes we have to shift our thinking. For me, I woke up and said, "Well, if not me, then who?" I accepted that, on this journey, for whatever reason, God has decided that he needs me to go through this. I embraced the fact that it's always bigger than me.

But again, anxiety is real, honey. Even the fear of pain is real. There were parts of me that worried about whether the biopsy would hurt. If there would be a lot of pain. But you know what? I didn't feel a thing. Honey, Tab almost took a nap on that table. So if I'd allowed my fear of the pain to work me up, it would have been for nothing.

One of the ways I was able to check the fear and anxiety that kept trying to come up was to remind myself that it wasn't just about me. As I said, it was bigger than me. I was going to use this as an opportunity to bring awareness about breast health to women like me. Yes, this is not the new thing I wanted to do, but I got through it and now God can use it. Worrying about it was never going to change anything. So honey, don't allow yourself to start worrying about something that doesn't exist yet. Fear, as we know, is false evidence appearing real. Be patient with yourself. Be willing to wait. Believe in good things and trust that God is in control because He always is.

And truth be told, that's growth for Tab. I cannot deny that going to the doctor is usually triggering for me because when I was sick before, I'd go all the time and they could never tell me what was wrong. So part of me is hesitant to even believe what a doctor says. Part of me wants to say, "Oh God, here we go again. Is something about to go wrong?" But the lesson God is giving me, and the one I want to share with you, is we all must check our triggers.

Triggers will happen, honey, especially on this healing journey. It's common to think you have gotten to a certain place in your healing, to say "Oh, I am good with this" and then be blindsided by a response in your mind or body that you didn't expect. That's a trigger! And the moment you find yourself saying "Oh, wait a minute, I thought I was good with this but I'm not!" is the moment to check your trigger. Do it right then! Because if you don't, it will become easier to slip back into old thoughts or ways.

And the truth is, that might not work, either. You just might backslide into your old thoughts and ways. Sometimes it's not until the damage is done and you find yourself thinking and acting out the way you used to that you get to the point where you actually realize you've been triggered in the first place. You might say, "Oh Lord, why did I go back to thinking that way? I know I'm better than this. I know I've grown past this." That's real! But honey, even if that's the case, don't you start tearing yourself down and feeling bad about yourself. Yes, you reacted to the trigger instead of checking it, but you are human. It happens. And thank God you know where you're supposed to be. You know what it feels like to be on the healing path, so you know how to put yourself back on it. So go on and do that. Say to yourself, "Okay, I didn't check myself when I should have. I messed up. I need to make amends with people I might have harmed in the process. But what I'm not going to do is beat myself up over it. That is not how I'm going to heal." And then get about the business of restoring yourself.

Healing is not beating ourselves up every time we respond to our triggers in a way that's not helpful. Healing is checking ourselves even when we mess up and doing what's necessary to move forward.

And some of what we might have to do to move forward is sit with our triggers for a bit.

When I got the news about my initial breast exam, I was forced to sit for a while with all those feelings that came up for me. There were a few weeks between the appointments and a whole holiday. So in that in-between time, I gave myself some time to sit with what was coming. Sometimes the parts of us that are scared just need to be heard. Sitting with those feelings allows them to be heard, and then you can get to talking back to them. You can check them by saying, "Yes, I see you, fear. Yes, I'm being affected by this thing that's happened. I acknowledge these feelings, but guess what? Tab, girl, don't you go there. Don't allow yourself to go back down into that old space just because of this one moment.

Because of this one small bit of information. You've done a lot of amazing healing. You've gotten your check-ups and done what you're supposed to do. Those are the only real facts you have right now. Don't allow this one moment to set you back." And when I did that, I was finally overwhelmed with such peace. But I had to sit with that thang first, y'all. Sitting with our triggers for a little bit helps us better break them down. It helps us understand ourselves just a little bit more. There ain't nothing wrong with taking your time with your triggers. In fact, that's a great way to continue to heal.

Remember, honey, healing is a journey. It's not permanent. We can still have triggers. But when they rise up in us, we should try to talk ourselves down off the ledge. I eventually received the amazing news from my doctors that I was all clear. There was nothing to worry about. Ooh God I thank you! But you know what? I was proud of how I handled it. Whereas the old Tab would have taken the news and literally given myself a death sentence, the new Tab, the healing Tab, sat with those feelings and then checked herself. I said, "No, ma'am, not today." So even as you are doing new things daily, and maybe those new things are bringing up some old stuff, some old ways, always be ready to check your triggers. Check those old versions of yourself that want you to react in old ways. You've been growing and healing, so even as these new things are stretching you, don't let your triggers set you back, alright? Check it and keep on going.

TSA
(Tabitha Service Announcement)

Don't wait until things feel too far gone.
Move on them now!

From Tab's "New Thing" Catalog

Make that doctor's appointment. You know that thing that you are afraid to find out about? It's time. Go ahead and find out what you need to do to heal.

Try some breathing exercises or yoga. Yoga can help you get back into your body; get to know it better.

Meditate to soft music for ten minutes, preferably spa music. There are thousands of guided meditation apps out there that can help you with this. They can even remind you to meditate at certain times of the day.

Meet My Play Cousin...
Michelle Did a New Thing

I don't do needles. At all. I jump and scream when I've had to get an IV at the hospital. So when a friend suggested that I try acupuncture, I was beyond hesitant. No, let me take that back— I was scared. All I kept imagining was a bunch of huge needles in my arms, legs, and back and that didn't sit well with me at all. But my back pain had gotten to the point where I was popping Tylenols every other day. If I didn't do something different, I was going to end up on much worse medication, or be forced to get regular steroid shots when things got really bad.

I did keep thinking about taking the leap and trying acupuncture because I knew at least three people who did and saw success. But if I'm honest, my fear kept me stuck. In fact, it was my fear that prevented me from even following up on a consultation that my friend recommended where I could ask questions and even see what a needle would feel like.

My fear was swiftly moved out of the way, though, when I threw my back out and was laid up in bed for almost a week. I missed work and pay and finally, I thought, enough is enough. I was going to have to do something new for all this to change. I needed to step outside my comfort zone, set my fears aside, and hope that this thing that everyone and their mama had told me about would work in helping me manage my pain. So I walked into the office of the acupuncturist my friend referred me to, and I immediately felt comforted. The practitioner gave me a detailed explanation of Eastern medicine and how it can work in conjunction with Western medicine, and then she brought out the needles.

I could barely feel them!

"Can I get a session now?" I asked. I felt such urgency in that moment.

The practitioner smiled and said, "Yes, I can do a short thirty-minute session before my next patient."

She was so accommodating as I laid on the table and walked through each step of the process. I closed my eyes and laid there as she touched my wrist while inserting needles in my back. When it was over, I was so stunned. The pain had lessened significantly. By the next day, I was walking and moving around almost normally.

The beautiful thing about now being on the other side of doing this new thing is knowing that had I not done it, I could have still been in pain or worse. Since my first session, I've seen a dramatic change in my body. No, the pain is not completely gone, but acupuncture has helped me deal with it so much better.

I know now that my resistance to doing something out of the box is usually driven by fear. And if I come across something else new to do, I will isolate the real issue and make my determination from there. If it's just fear, then I will decide if it's rational. I know now that I wasn't going to have a bunch of holes in my body causing me to bleed out. (Yes, that sounds ridiculous, but let's just say I have a very vivid imagination.) It was just my fear of the unknown holding me back, and if I can get myself to truly see that the benefits of a thing are greater than any potential negatives, then maybe it won't take me as long to make a move.

Nevertheless, I'm grateful for my new thing. I'm glad that I took a leap out there and I look forward to what I might do next. I feel like I now have the courage to try some other things that might be helpful for my back. I wonder what yoga is like.

Do Something for Someone Else

> "I have found that among its other benefits,
> giving liberates the soul of the giver."
> —*Maya Angelou*

I did a new thing.

As someone whose platform has grown in a mind-blowing way over the last few years, I meet so many new people and am always so grateful for all the support I receive. Honey, y'all don't play about Tab and I love it! But can I tell you what gives me the most joy? My heart swells so big when I'm able to give that love and support back to someone. People might call the followers I have "fans," but I like to think of every person behind an @ as family. I grew up in a small town—Eden, North Carolina—and always had a big family of real cousins, but I also have my play cousins. And that's how I see the people who show me love. We all cousins, y'all!

So when I had a chance to meet one of my play cousins today, it truly blessed me. I'd had the wonderful opportunity to visit *The Jennifer Hudson Show* once before, when my cookbook was released, but this time I wasn't going to promote anything. I wasn't going for me at all. The amazing host, JHud, was having Greta Onieogou from the hit television show *All-American* on, and a little birdie told me that she was a play cousin. Over the pandemic, Greta posted one of my recipes, and as I do sometimes, I responded to her and shared it on my Instagram story. Greta freaked out!

"Oh my God, we love you so much," she wrote to me.

And I did my share of freaking out, too.

"Oh my goodness, honey, my daughter and my husband watch the show and they love you!" I wrote back.

Now it was two years later, and Jennifer Hudson's team had reached out to see if I would send in a video surprise to Greta.

"Video? I am right down the street, honey, why would I send a video? Let me come on in there and give that baby a hug!"

And that's exactly what I did.

This was my first time ever surprising someone on network television, and I was so full. I felt so loved knowing that I was able to give back love in return. And it was so exciting! You know that anticipation you get when you know someone is going to be so happy. I had all the buzzing going on in my body as I waited to make my entrance. And when it was all over, God nudged me. He used this opportunity as a reminder that sometimes it's the simple things we do for others that matter. No, maybe you aren't surprising a play cousin on television, but you might be able to pop up on your granny so you can hug her neck and kiss her face. You might be able to surprise your baby with a trip to the ice cream parlor. You might be able to give your partner a much needed but unexpected massage after a tough day.

The thing is, we never know what kind of impact we can have on someone's life with just a small act of kindness. I got a chance to say hello to Greta, look her in her face, eye to eye, and tell her that I love her. I see her. That matters! Sometimes all you have to do is acknowledge someone and it changes the entire course of their day. And while it was new for me to do it on television in such a big way, I am recommitting myself to doing it more in my day-to-day life. I want to love harder, see deeper, and just be better. And if *you* want to love harder, you must be intentional. You must make room for people. Make space for them. Be patient with people and extend your ear, your time, your understanding, and your grace. Loving harder, by definition, means you must be open and willing to do that. Even when you think you've done enough, sometimes you just got to do a little bit more. That's just what it takes to make people feel seen.

When you are intentional about loving people on a regular basis, then you get real good at it. And honey, when you get good at it, you'll want to do it more and more. It gives me so much joy when I step in a room and people are in line and excited about meeting me. It's not an ego thing. It's just clear evidence that they feel loved by me. It's evidence that I'm doing something right.

TSA
(Tabitha Service Announcement)

*Remember, when we lie to make ourselves look
and feel better and the truth comes out,
we only look and feel worse. I love you.*

From Tab's "New Thing" Catalog

Buy or pick flowers and pass them out to random strangers.
You never know how that simple gesture might turn someone's day
around. Be the vessel that sends a hug or kiss from God to someone
who needs it.

Buy food or coffee for someone who's behind you in line.
Those unexpected, seemingly small blessings can help people keep
going.

Offer to cook or order out dinner for your partner. This is
especially a great "new thing" if you're the one who normally
doesn't cook.

Wear Something That Makes You Feel Good

"Baby, I feel good all over."
—*Stephanie Mills*

I did a new thing.

I'm so grateful to have a team of folks who help me do what I do. As someone who is on television and in other forms of media quite often, my makeup artist, Brandie, and hairstylist, Shaylin, have become like sisters to me. They not only keep both my face and Donna looking good, but they also stand ready to help me through long shoot days and the inevitable exhaustion that comes when the pace is busy. So today, as they were getting my glam ready for another appearance, they surprised me.

"We got a gift for you."

What?! I couldn't believe it.

"Oh my goodness, y'all didn't have to give me no gift."

But they did! And when I opened it, I couldn't help but to smile so big. Now honey, y'all know I love an avocado. Not only do I try to eat them every chance I get, I have avocado earrings, notebooks, pillows—you name it! I even hang out with an animated avocado named Avi on my children's show. So you can imagine how I felt when I opened the gift box and saw that my sisters had bought me an avocado jogging suit. Yes, a whole jogging suit with nothing but avocados on it.

"Oh my God, I love it! I've never had one of these before! I can't wait to wear it."

Honey, today I wore that avocado suit, ya' hear? And let me tell you something, that suit changed how I felt. I know it might seem like a funny or small thing, but wearing those avocados made me so happy. And I was happy all day long. People kept looking at me and saying, "Oh my God, look at your avocados!," and then they'd smile or laugh or otherwise be joyful. So not only did wearing my new avocado jogging suit make me happy, it brought joy to other people. Yes, maybe there was a person or two who was like "Look at this weird lady walking around with a full avocado jogging suit on," but I didn't care. These avocados were my business, and I loved every second of how they made me feel.

And isn't that just it?

When you wear your new thing today, do your best to set aside what other people might be thinking about it. Does it make you feel good? Does it make you happy? Are you overwhelmed with joy? Well then, that's your business, honey! And the wonderful side effect of focusing on doing something that makes you happy is that being intentional in this way opens the door for you to make someone else's day. Not because that's what you set out to do, but because joy is contagious, and when you're feeling good that can't help but to rub off on people you encounter along the way. My willingness to wear a full avocado suit made other people smile. So it did the job for me and, like only God can orchestrate, it did it for them, too. So honey, I encourage you to wear something that makes you happy and watch how that joy spreads.

And let me say this: if you are scared to do something as simple as wear what you want without caring what other people are going to say or think, then I'm going to encourage you to spend more time with yourself. You don't know who you are. You are afraid of you. That's the real truth. You might be saying that you are afraid of what other people might think, but really you are afraid of you. The power of you. There is uncertainty in who you are and what you want and/or like.

So get a little more comfortable with yourself, alright? If you feel comfortable in it, that's all that matters. Show up for you. Yes, you can be cute for your husband, your wife, or your partner. But you're supposed to show up for you first. You have got to love what you see in the mirror first.

Get to know *you*, baby. What do you like? What do you love? What do you need to feel well about you? Start unpacking those things, and I promise you'll get to a place where you don't care what people think about what you're wearing. As long as you love it and it feels good on you and you feel sexy or beautiful in it, honey, you ain't going to worry about what nobody else thinks. And, like I said, what they think ain't our business no way, right? Very good.

TSA
(Tabitha Service Announcement)

You are worthy of happiness!

From Tab's "New Thing" Catalog

Try some new accessories. If you tend to wear big earrings, then consider getting you some small studs, even some little diamonds. If you tend to wear no earrings or very small ones, honey, throw on some big hoops or something bright and colorful.

Change up your shoe game. Wear sneakers if you are always wearing heels. Throw on some stilettos if you stay in flats. (But honey, keep a pair of flats nearby in case you need them! Tab doesn't want you to hurt yourself.)

Bring the holidays to the regular days. Who doesn't love festive pajamas? You? Oh well, honey, let's switch things up. Do something new by throwing on some Christmas jammies or lounge wear in April. It's fun and might make you feel cozy—like you just gave yourself a big hug.

Meet My Play Cousin...
Tina Did a New Thing

I don't wear jeans. I have never worn jeans. Okay, so that's not entirely true. When I was a child and had no choice over the clothes I wore because my mother picked them out, I was forced to wear jeans. But when I became a teenager and started buying my own clothes, I never bought jeans. I'm a skirt girl. A dress girl. Even a shorts girl. But when it comes to jeans, I don't know, there's something about them that doesn't feel they are becoming on my body.

Part of me knows it's because I spent years listening to hip-hop and watching music videos in the nineties. Everything back then was about the big butt. The girls featured, the ones everyone called beautiful, had body shapes that were enhanced by jeans. The girls who wore jeans and had junk in the trunk got a lot of attention. And there was no junk to be had over here. As a matter of fact, my butt is as flat as a pancake. And whenever I put on jeans, it enhanced the butt I had and not the butt I wanted. For the longest time, that was enough for me to not wear jeans.

However, recently I was preparing for a family trip to Europe and needed to buy me some comfortable, casual clothes that would be durable enough for me to wear on all the bullet trains as we crisscrossed several countries. And yes, there are a million things I could have worn, but I had to admit that jeans just made sense for this kind of trip. Unfortunately, my body had not changed even after so many years. I still had the pancake booty, and the insecurities and self-consciousness that came with it. I knew going shopping for jeans would be torture.

Everyone told me that they now have jeans for all different types of bodies, but I was still skeptical. "That's fine and good," I said. "But will jeans look good on my body?"

I went into the first store and tried on some. I was not happy. They basically confirmed why I never wore jeans. But I didn't give up. I went to another store. Same deal. After the third store was a bust, I stopped to get something to eat. As I sat at the table, waiting for my burger, I pulled out my journal and began writing my feelings. That's when it happened. As I was writing, I had this overwhelming feeling come over me. It was like a voice was challenging all my insecurities. I heard God asking, "Why are you basing your entire wardrobe and its possibilities off an insecurity from your youth that's not even rooted in truth?" I wrote more about how this idea of a "pancake booty" was really a derogatory view of myself. I am a woman in my forties with a butt that was just fine.

And as I continued to write through my feelings, I started to cry. I mean, tears just flowed down my face and onto the page. But I allowed the words to come. I really had to let it all go. I had to purge myself of all these feelings that really weren't mine to have in the first place. It was society at large that said my body was not good enough. Not God. And not me. Not anymore. At the very end of my entry into my journal, I wrote over and over again: I am good enough. I am enough. I am enough. And then I shut the journal, finished my food, and went to the next store.

When I went to try on this next pair of jeans, I stood in the mirror for a long time. It was an amazing moment because, strangely, it was the first time that I was okay with what I saw. I was okay with what my butt looked like in those jeans. It was as if that conversation between God and myself affirmed me and gave me the strength to see myself in a new light. When I looked in the mirror, I didn't see the same body and the same person I had just seen hours ago when my eyes were clouded by negativity.

That was it. I took those jeans to the counter, and did something I hadn't done in many years, something that was incredibly new for this adult version of myself. I bought a pair of jeans. Then I took them home, packed them in my bag, and wore them many, many times on my trip in Europe.

Do Something That Helps You Find Light in Darkness

"Hope is being able to see that there is light
despite all of the darkness."
—*Archbishop Desmond Tutu*

I did a new thing.

I know many people see me smiling and laughing on their
screens, and it can be easy to believe I have no hard days. That
my life is nothing but sunshine and avocados. To be clear, I love
my life. I love what God does daily to show me just how much He
loves me. I'm so grateful for every opportunity I have. But I am
human. I have good days and bad days and sometimes downright

ugly days. Today has been a tough one. I just learned about the death of dancer, choreographer, and all-around beautiful soul DJ Twitch by suicide.

I woke up this morning already emotional. I attended my son's last holiday performance in elementary school, and I guess it was dawning on me just how fast time flies. It seems like yesterday I was looking down at him in my arms and now he will be heading off to middle school. So the mama tears were already in their full glory when I got the news about Twitch. That sent them into a full waterfall.

I actually allowed this loss to affect me. I sat in the sadness for a bit. I prayed for Twitch's family and others who have been impacted by suicide, including my own family (I love you, Jen and Carlos). I prayed for my son as I reflected on him growing up. I know how easily the world can influence him as he enters middle school. As I came out of prayer, I felt God's presence and heard God's voice: "You have more work to do, Tab. More light to spread and more love to give. It's needed now more than ever." And with that, I pulled myself together and prepared for my shoot!

Honey, God pressed that one message into my heart.

And I don't think that was meant to disregard my sorrow or to take away the real feelings I have as a mother watching her baby boy grow up. But it is a reminder that life is short and while I'm still here, I can use my time to spread love. I can still spread joy. And that's exactly what I decided to do with the rest of my day. Despite the grief I was feeling this morning, I told my team that I would go ahead with the scheduled photo shoot.

I'm so glad I did.

The photo shoot was for an independent publication, *Cheryl Magazine,* owned by a wonderful woman I'd met the previous summer, Cheryl Williamson. I'll never forget meeting this gorgeous woman with beautiful gray locs for the first time. After a brief conversation, my assistant, Hope, and I both said the same thing: "This woman feels like family!" And she did. There was an instant connection there. Over the last year, we kept running into Cheryl at other events, and it got to the point when we knew that it wasn't a coincidence that we kept running into each other. During the last encounter, we finally exchanged contact information, and she said, "I created my own magazine, and my prayer one day is to have you in it."

I said, "Well, let me do one better for you. I ain't going to be in it. I'm going to be on your cover."

Then she started to cry. "Oh my goodness, would you really do something like that?"

"Absolutely."

And when we saw each other again at one of the stops on my book tour, I made a point to remind her, "Honey, I'm going to be on your cover. Let's make sure we make it happen. I don't want us to put it off." And she cried again.

Well, our teams made it happen. Today, I did a full photo shoot with Cheryl, and she was so happy. I felt so full just seeing her tears of joy and confirmation. Her tears were clearly evidence that when God says He's going to do something, He's going to do it. But I also realized that God was doing something in me today also. I had been trying to force myself to feel happy all morning. My grief was heavy. And simply by showing up to the photo shoot, my spirits were lifted. I felt like I was doing something right in the world. I found light even in the darkness.

Here's the thing: I don't know Ms. Cheryl personally, but I suspect by the way she cried that she must have gone through some things. None of us know what the Twitches of the world are going through as they are navigating the dark spaces our minds can too often take us to. Honey, I've been to those dark places, there's nothing fun about it. But the one thing that we can do for anyone we know who's in those places is try to be their light. I walked into that photo shoot after crying my eyes out that morning and praying for strength, having decided to go and be a light for Cheryl and her magazine. And because I chose to be light, I watched in real time the light come over her.

Doing this magazine shoot was my new thing today. I support small businesses all the time, but this was the first time I was led to support in this way! The whole time I was smiling and posing, I was also remembering that this is exactly what light is supposed to do.

Those who know me and my work know that I champion positivity. I believe in normalizing positivity. I'll never forget this TikTok video done not too long ago that said that I represented toxic positivity. When I first saw the video, the first thing I thought was "Oh man, the pain this person must be in." Sadly, there are people who are in such a dark place that they find authentic positivity, of all things, toxic. It's a scary thought for me, but that's how real the darkness is for some. It can get so dark in our lives that we think it's the only way to see. Nevertheless, every day I try to be intentional with being light.

Honey, our light is *supposed* to shine. It's supposed to push out the darkness. First within ourselves and then in others. During and after the photo shoot, we all danced, and through movement, I allowed myself to release my sadness in that moment. No, I didn't forget about what was happening; what had happened. But even when we are hit with bricks of sadness and emotion, we can choose to use those bricks to build safety for ourselves and other people. That safe space allows us to push through and shine our light even through the cracks. Yes, we do it for ourselves. Yes, it's important for our own healing. But we also have the power to do it for those around us who need it. Those who don't have the energy to pick up their bricks. I could have gotten caught up in the darkness. I could have canceled the photo shoot because the pain was too much. But I didn't. I absolutely felt everything. I cried. I hurt. I allowed myself some time with those emotions. But I didn't stay there. I pulled myself out of it and found my light.

I know that's not easy for everybody. I'm not saying that it is. But when you can, when you're dealt a dark hand, try your best to find your light and pull yourself up. Feel around the walls of that pain until you can get to the switch that will turn your light back on.

We can all be intentional about spreading joy, laughter, love, and happiness, even when we're having bad days. Sometimes just showing up can help someone else out of a dark place. Honey, sometimes just showing up will help *you* out of a dark place. Just like it did for me today with the photo shoot. So yes, positivity is a huge part of my purpose, and ain't nothing toxic about it. God has asked me to be a light for people—especially those who don't know how to find their way out of darkness. I get to show them through my life and testimony that one day, minute, second at a time, they can make it. Because I did.

And sometimes it's just a simple acknowledgment that changes a person's day. Walking around a grocery store, saying hello, and looking folks in the eyes can be a game-changer. Embracing people and asking how they are doing—and really meaning it—can change someone's day. Whatever that seemingly small thing is, it can make a big difference in how someone feels about their own darkness, their journey, even their life. So in the grand scheme of things, yes, normalize positivity. Let's think more positively than we do negatively. For those who are struggling, we can be their gentle reminder that it's going to get better.

TSA
(Tabitha Service Announcement)

You have the power to be a light in dark places.

From Tab's "New Thing" Catalog

Light a new candle. Get a new, warm scent that can really settle you down. Maybe like a shea vanilla with a little bit of lavender, which might help you get your balance.

Journal about your feelings. Sometimes it's best to get any negative feelings outside of you by writing them on the paper. And then the most important part—after you journal, read what you wrote out loud so that it helps get the thoughts associated with those bad feelings out of your head.

Watch a comedy or a stand-up special. Laughter is a form of self-love. When you give yourself room to just laugh, it may allow you to get a little bit of light in your dark time or day.

Do Something That Challenges What You *Think* You Know

"Transformation is often more about
unlearning than learning."
—*Richard Rohr*

I did a new thing.

I went on a private school tour with my son and husband.

Growing up in Eden, there were no private schools. Honey, the town was so small that everyone went to the same middle and high school no matter where you lived. So to be honest, it has been difficult for me and my husband to wrap our minds around sending our son to a private middle school next year. Sure, living in

Los Angeles means that we know plenty of people whose children attend private school, but it still wasn't something that we ever thought we'd consider for our own children.

Before agreeing to go on the tour, I sat with myself for a bit to evaluate why I was having such a difficult time with this decision. What I figured out was that I had attached some negative thoughts to private school. You see, somewhere in my mind I had convinced myself that people who sent their children to private school thought they were better than those who went to public school. And in my heart, I worried that people might think we thought that way, too. In truth, Tab was just scared. Afraid of how the decision would be perceived by those who have known us forever.

But listen, if I'm going to live free and profess that freedom every day to those who support me, then I knew I had to take a beat to change the way I was thinking about this. I had to separate the views I had about private school that were not based on anything I'd actually ever experienced from the bottom-line truth: By sending my child to private school, I'm simply giving him another opportunity. One that I wish I could have possibly had.

Fortunately, we are able to provide this for him, so why not? Plus, in a way, it's something we'd been doing already. Our daughter, Choyce, had attended a Christian preschool, and we paid for it out of pocket. There was no government funding. No school district regulations. So how was this any different, Tab?

It wasn't.

But honey, even as we entered them school doors today, the anxiety was still there. I was worried, for sure, but I was also willing to put that worry aside to see what was possible. And baby, the possibilities blew my and my husband's minds. Walking through those hallways and seeing all the different things my son could be exposed to was such an awakening for me. All I could think was *Wow. If my parents had the opportunity, they probably would've chosen this for me, too.*

I remember as a kid, sharing my dreams of becoming an actress with my parents. I'd say, "I really want to pursue acting when I grow up, Moma. I want to go to Hollywood, Daddy." And I also distinctly remember them saying, "We support you. We just don't know how to help you get there." My parents didn't have the resources or the knowledge, but I do.

The thing about the private school we visited today is they have an athletic program that's geared toward basketball. My son loves basketball. He has said for many years, even as a little bitty boy, that he wants to play it professionally. And this school has a program that helps student-athletes prepare for exactly that. Listening to the administrators talk, I couldn't help but think about where I might be now if I could have gone to a private school where acting was part of the core curriculum. If I can put Quest in an environment where other kids are also focused on basketball, then he will have a village that he can thrive in. He doesn't have to fight against people who may not have the same goals. He will be able to work hard within a system that can support his dreams while also getting a well-rounded, top-notch academic education. What more can a mama want? Why would I hold that back from my baby boy because of my own hang-ups about how it would be perceived? No, ma'am—it was time to change my thinking.

While I had to unlearn some things I believed about private

school, this unlearning applies to so many different areas of our lives. For many of us who grew up in church, we've often had to unlearn and relearn some things that don't ring true for us in our spirits now that we are grown and have lived a little bit. For example, I remember being taught as a child that if I didn't go to church every Sunday, then God would not be pleased with me and I could be hellbound. But y'all know that Little Tab had questions, right? I'd ask things like: Well, what about people who have to work on Sundays? What about people who are bedridden or sick in the hospital and they can't get to church? Are they going to go to hell? What about people who never heard of Christianity? Are they really going to hell because no one taught them this? In my childlike mind I didn't understand why God would not be okay with them not coming to church. And honey, I still don't.

So grown-up Tab took that trauma—and that's how I see it—and I began working to shake myself loose from it. That was and is part of my healing process. In fact, I heard from God very early on in this freedom walk of mine, and He clearly said: "Listen, forget about all that you were taught. I want you to focus on what you feel. I'm showing you what I'm building and developing inside of you. Listen to me as I speak to you in your heart." After that word, it was a wrap! Removing those layers of poor or inadequate teaching has led to me working day by day to heal and unlearn. Sometimes I get it right. Other days, well, those old teachings sure do know how to rear their ugly heads.

I remember going home to Eden with my family recently and going to visit my daddy's church. My daughter, Choyce, brought a sundress to wear; a long maxi dress with spaghetti straps. Of course it was beautiful on her, but without even thinking, I said, "Girl, wait one minute. What are you wearing?"

"What?" she said.

"You can't wear that dress."

"Why?" she asked.

And that's when I had to take a minute. You see, my mind had reverted back to those old teachings. I was thinking, *You can't show no arms in church, Girl. You need to cover up.*

Then she said something that brought me back. "Mommy, you are treating me the same way you said you hated to be treated growing up."

She was right. And I told her as much. I apologized for unconsciously transferring those old thoughts to her. Allowing people, sometimes even our children, to hold us accountable for our growth is major. Yes, sometimes we'll be inclined to fight against it, and I could have been mad at her for pointing out my hypocrisy, but I decided to sit with it for a minute and say to myself, *Yes, Tab, you are projecting. That ain't right.*

So no, honey, unlearning isn't easy. Whether it's thoughts on private school, outdated religious practices, or something else, we all have a responsibility to reevaluate what we believe and to pay attention to how God may be changing what you think about a thing. Maybe you have to remove yourself from something all together until you can get your mind right. That's okay, too. There are different ways to do it, but when we decide to make that shift, it can be both a blessing and a relief.

This new thing I did today—visiting the private school—really made me check myself and those old thoughts. I had to remind myself that I was on new land. I was in new territory with this blessed life of mine, and with that new territory there needs to be a new mindset. I have to keep my mind open to what God wants to do and not allow my old mind to put up obstacles that might block me and my family's future blessings. As we left the school today, I said to myself, "This is why you're here, Tab. You've worked very hard for this." And I have. Both my husband and I have worked so hard to get to a place where we can support our children, not just financially, but also support them in their growth and the pursuit of their dreams. Too many times, we don't give ourselves credit for that hard work because we are so busy being worried about what somebody else might think. But honey, I say who cares? What other people think about me and you ain't none of our business.

How about you accept whatever God has given you as the blessing, but also try to unlearn all those thoughts you used to think have no bearing on your present-day life. How about we all stop forming opinions about things we know nothing about. Allowing God to open our minds and hearts to something new will always benefit us and those we love.

TSA
(Tabitha Service Announcement)

Being scared of the unknown is a normal emotion,
but devaluing the unknown is ignorance.

From Tab's "New Thing" Catalog

Learn a new word. Go to a dictionary and find a word you have never used before. Then use the word throughout your day. This way, you challenge yourself by expanding your vocabulary. Maybe even help expand others by asking people, "You ever heard this word before?"

Read an autobiography or watch a documentary. Honey, we can learn so much from other people's lives. Their stories can both inspire you or give you courage. You might learn something you never knew, and it's another great way to challenge yourself.

Sit in on a public court hearing. I know this might seem strange, but I've actually done this back in the day. I actually ended up there by accident, but I remember being young and saying, "You know what? I want to come and do that again." You learn so much about people. If you have a day where you can just go and sit and watch how court is run—it's easier to do in small towns—give it a try. It's actually very interesting to learn how our laws work and how people get sentenced. You also hear the crazy things people say. Just think of it as people watching on steroids.

'Do Something That Breaks the Rules (but, Honey, Not the Law)

"If you obey all the rules, you miss all the fun."
—*Katharine Hepburn*

I did a new thing.

I disregarded the dress code at a swanky party.

Now, if there is one thing y'all know about Tab, it's that I love me some color. I will wear yellow, orange, green, and blue, all at the same time if I want to, because that's my business. So when I received the invitation to attend an exclusive party for a well-known superstar performer, I was ready to do what I do. Unfortunately, as I read further, I found out that there was a specific dress code. They were encouraging guests to wear futuristic outfits and preferably all black.

Honey, Tab don't do black.

I *really* don't like wearing black. It doesn't make me happy. For some reason, I don't like how wearing black makes me feel. Yes, I know what people say: Black is chic and sophisticated. Black makes you look thinner. That's all fine and good. But I am a woman who happily rocked an avocado suit because it made me smile. If something doesn't feel good to me, I can't wear it. Especially not *all* black. If I happen to wear a black suit, trust and believe I'm going to have a pop of color somewhere. And most of the time, I won't even do that. The idea of wearing all black makes me feel sad and heavy. And who wants to feel that way at a party?

So that was my dilemma today. I really wanted to go to this party but I didn't want to adhere to the dress code. I tried to find something that would be a compromise—something that would still fall into the theme of the event but wouldn't require me to wear all black. And honey, I did it! I found the perfect outfit! After going through a few pieces, I landed on some black velvet bell-bottom pants that were super cute, which I paired with a suit jacket that had these sharp pointed sleeves. The structure of the blazer was very space-like but the fabric was colorful like I like it. The rich colors of blue, burgundy, and gold . . . and yes, with a tiny bit of black . . . made me feel so good. As I was trying on the outfit, I remember thinking to myself, *This is going to have to work.* And honey, it surely did. Tab looked fabulous. And why? Yes, the outfit was cute and Donna was doing what Donna does, but more than anything, I felt fabulous because I chose myself. I wore something that felt like me. See, I still need to feel happy when I walk into a room, especially if it's a party, which should be festive and fun anyway. And black was never going to make me feel that way. So breaking the rules, within reason, was always going to be what was best for me in this instance. I went against the ask, and I wasn't going to apologize for that at all.

And guess what, y'all? Sure enough, when we got there, there were other people who didn't have on all black, either. Thank God I chose me, right?

That's what I want you to take away from this today. I think it's 100 percent okay to not always do exactly what someone asks of you, at least when it comes to something like this. Sure, if there are strict rules on the job or if resisting will cause unnecessary problems for you or someone else, then you might want to use wisdom. *Maybe.* But even then, I still say to be sure that what's being asked doesn't conflict with your freedom!

Tab is certainly not saying to blow up your life because you don't want to wear black. Don't y'all run out here saying I told y'all to break the law. But there are plenty of scenarios where we do things that make us feel terribly uncomfortable all because we are afraid to be ourselves and go against the grain. If you are asked to do something, but you know it will take something out of you or it is something that doesn't make you feel good, then honey, you have every right to break the rules or, if the rules can't be broken, choose not to go to that place or do that thing. Every invitation does not have to be accepted. And honey, every invitation ain't our responsibility. The only responsibility you really have is to yourself. To your own heart and mind and soul. I say this all the time, but I'm not sure folks hear me: *put yourself first.*

I know that goes against conventional advice. Especially to women. But if I don't make myself comfortable, the truth is, nobody else will. If I ain't treating me well, somebody else ain't going to really know what *well* means to me. This opens the door for people to treat me any old way they want.

So yes, I'm talking about breaking rules, but really it's bigger than that. It's about shifting your focus to what's going to make you feel most yourself and never, ever deviating from that. It's not selfish to take care of yourself. It's not selfish to wear what makes you feel good. You don't ever have to apologize for choosing to make yourself feel good over some rules that likely don't matter in the grand scheme of things anyway. Take the time to make sure you are safe within yourself—and watch how even the people, places, and things around you change for your good. Today, I did a new thing by choosing to show up in a way that makes me feel good first and foremost. And I realize that this is what it means to be truly free. To make those decisions, own those decisions, and never apologize for it.

So, honey, what rules are you breaking today?

TSA
(Tabitha Service Announcement)

Making your own rules is true freedom!

From Tab's "New Thing" Catalog

Speak your truth. If you're in a situation today where something doesn't feel right, or maybe there's something you've been wanting to say but haven't, go ahead and speak what's in your heart. Yes, they might be expecting you to be quiet. But you're doing something new today.

Practice silence. Maybe you're the person who is always mouthing off. Maybe you are the one always sharing your opinion. Well, today, decide to not do that. Do a new thing by saying nothing. Keep it to yourself.

Get a canvas and paint a picture. Push past whatever ideas you might have about what an artist is. Tap into your artistry today, even with just an easy DIY craft project. So many people discover new hobbies and talents by simply wandering into a craft store and taking something home.

Meet My Play Cousin...
Stacy Did a New Thing

So, my new thing is something I never thought I would ever do. I'm not sure I ever really wanted to do it. As a matter of fact, whenever I heard about people taking solo vacations out of the country, I thought they were crazy. Sure, do a staycation or take a train to the next city over, but get on a plane and actually leave the country alone? No ma'am. All I could think about were all the lessons I'd been given about traveling alone as a woman. It didn't seem safe and, frankly, it never occurred to me that it was something I would really enjoy. But I kept hearing over and over from my friends and acquaintances about how freeing it is to travel alone, and since life has just been hitting me left and right lately, I knew I needed to do something that was going to give me a new perspective, or even just allow me to rest on my own terms.

A lot of times when you go on vacation with other people or with a boyfriend, you're sort of stuck doing an itinerary that maybe you didn't want to do. Or it's harder to change your mind because there's more than one person to consider. By booking this solo trip, I was hoping that I could just have some freedom, and man, did I ever!

I took a flight from Atlanta to Fort Lauderdale and then to St. Thomas in the U.S. Virgin Islands. I don't know if I can explain it, but as soon as I landed on the island, I felt a weight lift off me. It was like everything that I was going through, everything I'd left behind, had gone away. I am so glad I took the leap of faith and booked this trip.

First, I did so many things I never would've done had I gone with any friend of mine, including one day where I just sat in the room all day long and ate candy (my favorite is TWIX) and deep-dish pizza, courtesy of the all-inclusive resort I was staying in. Another day I ran into a woman who was also on a solo trip, although it was clearly something she'd done quite often. We hit it off great. She was from Chicago, but we worked in similar fields, and honestly, it did my soul so good to make a new friend. As a matter of fact, after spending the entire day on the white sand beach, alternating between reading novels and taking dips in the clear, turquoise water, me and my new homegirl spent the evening in the resort's movie theater, watching movies, eating popcorn, and drinking wine like Olivia Pope from the TV show *Scandal*. We had an absolute blast!

It's highly likely that had I not gone on this trip alone, I never would have met her. It never would have occurred to me to even hang out with someone I didn't know. But I did, and I'm so grateful. Sometimes when we get an opportunity to try new things, out of fear we don't do them. We think that somehow *that thing* is for somebody else or we are not the "type" of person who does that. But that's not how it works. The truth is, you never know what type of person you really are until you try the new thing. Plus, who wants to be the same person they've been for years and years all because we won't try anything new? I don't. And that's why I'm now planning on taking at least one solo trip every year for the foreseeable future.

'Do Something That Brightens (and Maybe Transforms) Someone's Day

"No act of kindness, no matter how small,
is ever wasted."
—*Aesop,* The Lion and the Mouse

I did a new thing.

I taught my son how to pay it forward.

Y'all know that sometimes Tab can just sense things. It's a gift God has given me. To not react immediately, but to discern what a situation might call for and move forward only when I'm clear. That's what I think happened today. Quest and I arrived at Subway, the sandwich chain, to pick up some of our favorite subs. Another woman arrived around the same time. If you've been in one of these kinds of assembly-line type of restaurants, where the employees are making your food right in front of you, then you know that sometimes depending on the size of the order or if you haven't decided which toppings you want, the person behind you might move ahead of you in line. Because we only had two sandwiches and she had quite a few, they called us down the line to pick up our food while still preparing hers. Apparently, she wasn't too happy about that.

I noticed that the woman was getting really frustrated about the fact that we'd gone ahead of her, even though there wasn't too much we could do about that. So I told my son, "You see, she was here first, but now we are in front and that seems to be upsetting for her. Whenever you can, it's good to meet a person's frustration with compassion instead of ignoring their feelings. Mommy is going to offer to pay for her food."

"But why?" Quest asked.

"Because you just never know what a person is going through. Maybe she has a limited amount of time for lunch. Or sometimes when people are made second, or someone is allowed to go in front of them, it can trigger a memory of something that happened a long time ago. Or maybe today has just been a hard one for her. Doing something nice just might change the course of her day. Mommy could be wrong, but right now Mommy's heart feels like we should offer to pay. It feels good and right for Mommy to do that."

And in his nonchalant way, he accepted that. "Okay, Mom."

But I wanted to add another important piece to this unexpected teachable moment.

"But we always want to make sure that people know we're being respectful," I continued. "When we pay it forward, we want people to know that we are doing so out of kindness, not because we are looking down on them or have any expectations of them."

"Got it," he said.

So I turned to the cashier and asked if the woman had finished ordering.

"Yes, I think this is her entire order," the cashier said.

Then I looked at the woman and asked, "Would it be okay for me to pay for your food today? I saw that you were here before us, and honey, we weren't trying to jump in front of you. Our food just got done a bit quicker."

The look on the woman's face was unforgettable. It was like she went from frustration to a full out exhale in a few seconds. "Oh my goodness, thank you so much!"

Notice she didn't say, "Oh, you don't have to do that." She didn't say anything but thank you. It was clear to me she was relieved as all the tension had drained from her face. Again, I don't know what she was going through, but I did sense that our small bit of kindness might have just made her day better. And more than anything, I wanted Quest to see that, too.

When we got in the car, I asked my son, "Did you see how she began to smile? How she took that deep breath as if she was released from something?"

"Yeah," he said.

"A simple act of kindness is all that's needed sometimes," I said.

Here's the thing, y'all: No, you don't always have to do it. Sometimes you might not be able to. But when you can, choose to brighten someone's day. And guess what? You just might brighten yours, too. And we don't always need a reason to pay it forward or be nice. Sometimes the act of doing so is just instinctual, and we do it without expectation of something in return.

As we pulled out of the lot, Quest said, "I feel cool, Mom."

"Well, feeling cool about doing love work is a great way to feel, Bud."

And honey, that's when it clicked. Today's new thing wasn't just about helping this woman. It was about what I was teaching my son. He'd seen me give money to the homeless before, but this was the first time I'd ever taught him how to actually interact in kindness with strangers. Now he's super excited about doing good deeds, and that makes his mommy feel really good.

Listen, honey, considering the world we are living in, compassion is probably the thing that's going to keep us all alive. So many of us are moving through life in such an angry state. There's this debating spirit nowadays where people will argue about just anything. Feels like there's a competition to see who can say or do the meanest, most hurtful thing. It's a really interesting time in the world. But compassion is free. It costs nothing to be kind to somebody. I truly believe this is what we were all meant to do: to see and love each other. And the truth is, when we show someone love and compassion, we just might be the only person who's done that for them in the entire day, week, or year.

We're all living on this earth together and because I think God intended for us to be compassionate toward each other, I know that the one and only way we are going to ensure that compassion continues is if we teach our children how to love. How to care. How to be a light for somebody else. They have to not only hear us tell them to be this way, but they must see us *being* that way. We have to be good models of compassion, first and foremost. Remember, those same children grow up to be adults, and if we don't teach them compassion as children, baby, when they get older we cannot complain about them being hell on wheels. So today, let's try to make the world a better place, one person at a time.

TSA
(Tabitha Service Announcement)

You may not be where you desire to be in life,
but you're always in a position to be kind.

From Tab's "New Thing" Catalog

Share with a child something they've taught you—Children get so excited when they know they've taught their parents something. Too many times our kids feel so small, but when you validate them and say "You know what? I learned this from you," it's a great way to lift their spirits and make their day.

Send balloons or flowers to a loved one's job or to the school. Ain't nothing like the feeling of administrators at school calling our name out over the speaker or getting an email saying that there was a gift in the main office for us.

Tell a cashier you appreciate them. When you go into a store or restaurant, simply letting a service worker know they are seen can make them feel so good. And it will make you feel good, too!

Do Something Hard but Necessary

"Just because something made you happy in the
past doesn't mean you have to keep it forever."
—*Melva Green*

I did a new thing.

When Chance and I put down roots in Los Angeles, it was very
important to us to have a village. We—well, y'all know Chance, it
was mostly me—wanted to create close relationships like we were
familiar with back home. I believe there is power in the chosen
family. They may not be the people who are related to you by
blood, but they're people who you've shared a kind intimacy with
and you treat just like family.

And I did just that. Over the course of fifteen years, our village grew into a group of individuals who were tight knit and looked out for each other. We even had our own chat thread where we'd discuss what was in our hearts that day and what was going on in our lives. It's how I invited everyone to my house for Sunday dinners, parties, vacations, or whatever the case. It was how we stayed connected.

Over time, though, I began to notice that the group dynamic was changing. I found myself being the only one who was constantly trying to keep this group of people together, and it felt like I was forcing relationships with people who, for whatever reason, didn't want to be close to me anymore. A part of me realizes that as I became more successful, some of those in our village might have felt like they couldn't relate to me anymore. Or maybe there was unacknowledged jealousy or envy there. But honey, Tab still tried to keep everyone together. I did everything I knew how to do to let these people know that no matter what was happening in my life and career, I was the same Tab who loved and cared for them. But it didn't work. There were some underhanded things happening and specific relationships didn't feel the same.

"Listen, sometimes you have to be ready to close a chapter in your life, no matter how amazing it used to be."

God had spoken. He placed it in my heart to let some of the relationships within my village go. But honey, I didn't want to. I really didn't. It hurt. But I know better than to not be obedient. People had changed, as people do. And if I was totally honest, I *wasn't* the same Tab. I certainly wasn't the same Tab I was fifteen years ago. I had grown. I was healing. And because of that, my new thing today was to be honest and transparent about how I was feeling, and to send a message to that same, long-standing chat thread essentially stating that I was closing the door and the chapter on these relationships.

Please understand that this is something I never thought I'd do. Never thought I *could* do. But I knew that I should if for no other reason than God told me to. And y'all, guess what? As soon as I sent the message, it felt like a ton of bricks had just lifted right on off me. Honey, I could breathe better. That's how I know it was a weight I was not supposed to carry.

Now, do I still feel the pain of loss? Absolutely. I probably will for a long time. I keep thinking about the holidays and how I'd normally be celebrating with some of these same people. But I have to trust God and believe that He knows what's best for me. That He is protecting me. Yes, it was one of the best, most fun chapters of life. But it's a closed one now.

Honey, Tab, is not going to sit here and pretend like intentionally letting someone close to you go doesn't hurt. All the times I've had to do this, it definitely still pains me. And I think what hurts the most is that I thought the relationships were more than they were. So many times we have to decide to let someone go not because something has dramatically changed but because we finally realize that we've had this person in the wrong place in our lives all along. It's not easy to accept that we've been treating a work friend like a bestie, and that's probably *why* there was no reciprocation in the relationship. There's some shame in the mix there. So when you do finally make a move, the real pain can come from admitting to yourself that you got it wrong.

If you are going through this, please give yourself some grace.

The healing process takes time. There are things I used to do with my former friends that I will miss doing. We used to hit the spa together or travel, and all of that's gone. On the days when I begin to hurt over that, I try to allow myself to feel the grief of that in the moment, while still making sure I stick to what's right for me.

Also, one of the hardest parts about letting go will be staying committed to the clean break. I'm a "reach out and see how you are doing" type of person. So not being able to do that with people I once loved is really hard. But every time I broke that commitment to myself, when I sent that quick check-in text, I found out the hard way that my reaching out was a wasted effort. It rarely ever served me well to reach out, especially before there has been healing.

Can there be reconciliation with someone you've let go? Of course there can be. But not if there is no healing done on both parts. And truth be told, you'll have to weigh the risks that will inevitably come from reconnecting and trying to figure out whether the person has actually changed. For me, as long as my heart holds no malice for the person, I don't necessarily feel a need to bring a person I've let go back into my life. There are no ill feelings. I don't wish anyone I've had to release any ill will. As a matter of fact, I wish them all the love and joy they can stand. But I've committed to living a free life and part of that is not engaging in one-sided relationships in which I'm doing all the pouring out and nobody is pouring in.

You know, that's one thing I realize about success. The more successful you get, the less people want to pour into you. They think you don't need anything. They believe you have it all together when sometimes, most times, that's far from the truth.

The more successful we are, the more we need to be checked on. With me, people see the glitz and glam of television shows and video shoots, but they don't see the twenty-hour days and sleepless nights. They don't see the planes, trains, and automobiles, honey. They don't see the ugly parts even when I love what I do. This life can be exhausting and heavy, especially for someone like me who loves people and is constantly encountering all kinds of spirits and energies all the time. I have to make sure that with those close to me, I am protecting my peace. Protecting my energy. So I'm grateful to have a handful of people who still check on Tab and make sure I'm good.

Maybe letting go of a friend or family member is not the hard new thing you need to do today. Maybe it's letting go of an old way of thinking. Maybe it's releasing a habit or behavior that's not serving you well or is causing you much heartache. Whatever it is, be obedient to what you know you must do and trust that in the long run, it will work out for your good.

TSA
(Tabitha Service Announcement)

Love has the ability to give you the best hug and the worst pain. However, I will always choose it!

From Tab's "New Thing" Catalog

Learn the Heimlich maneuver or take a CPR class. Yes, it can be hard, but it might be necessary to save someone's life one day.

Pamper yourself. Honey, I love a good spa, but sometimes the best spa days are the ones I do from home. Put a face mask on, throw some cucumbers on your eyes, and soak in the tub. I'm always blown away by how many people never soak in a tub or haven't in the last five, ten, or twenty years.

Create an at-home first-aid or emergency kit. This is so good to have! Put in your container all the things you think your family might need and place it somewhere convenient that everybody knows about.

Meet My Play Cousin . . .
Christine Did a New Thing

Every morning, I'd wake up, sit on the edge of my bed, and breathe a deep heavy sigh. I guess that should have been my first sign, huh? I had such a hard time getting myself together to get ready to go to work. That wasn't always the case, though.

When I first took the job working in the development office at a large nonprofit organization five years ago, I hopped out of bed so fast. I was excited about the new opportunity. But now my stomach turns into knots as soon as I pull into the parking lot. When I walk into the office, those knots tighten their grip and my chest starts to ache. Sometimes it feels like my heart is going to beat out of my chest. My job was literally making me sick, and for the longest time I had no idea what to do about it.

I think it was a combination of things. I had a supervisor who lacked empathy and compassion. Three years into my position, I lost my mother unexpectedly. I came in about fifteen minutes late the day after the funeral, and this woman had the audacity to say to me that I shouldn't be late because "people lose their mothers all the time. That's not an excuse!" That was a huge turning point for me, because it was in that moment when I realized it wasn't a safe place. It wasn't a place where I could or wanted to grow.

As much as I loved doing the work I did, it didn't feel worth it after a while. The chest pains had recently progressed to numbness in my feet and hands. I'd gone to the doctor multiple times over the last few months, only for them to run all the tests they possibly could and tell me that it was likely stress and anxiety. My blood pressure was regularly high. If I stayed at this job, I knew it would take me out. Yet, as many of us do, I rationalized it. *I have bills to pay. I have a mortgage. I have family members I'm responsible for; I am a caregiver. I'm active in my community and in my church.* All of that meant, in my mind, that I had to have a job. And that was true. I needed a job. I'm just not sure I needed *that* job. I was increasingly beginning to realize that it was time to do a new thing and make a shift. I had to trust that God would take care of me in the meantime.

So last week I walked into that office, felt those same knots in my stomach, and had the same panicky feelings. I sat at my desk for a little bit and felt my feet go numb. Then I slowly but surely began putting my papers, laptop, and my favorite books into the extra bag I'd brought that day. I opened the Amazon box I'd brought from home and put my flowers and pictures of my mother in my bag. Then I printed out on the desktop computer the letter I had written the night before, placed it in an envelope, and walked to my boss's office. Of course, when she saw me standing in the doorway, she looked slightly annoyed. That's okay, though, because I knew this was the last time I'd ever have to annoy her. I handed her my resignation.

"So you're not going to give two weeks' notice?" she said.

I thought about what my body had gone through for the last five years. What the last couple of months had felt like. I decided that two weeks was two weeks too long for my body to deal with what I dealt with.

"No," I said.

Then I turned around, picked up my things in my office, and walked out the door.

Now I'm not necessarily advising people to quit the way I did. But at some point we all have to evaluate whether or not the risk we are taking by staying is worth it, whether the pain of staying is greater than the pain of leaving. No, I don't have another job yet. I have some opportunities on the horizon but nothing set in stone. But here's what I do know: when I walked out of the doors of that office, the knots just completely unraveled in my body. There was such a relief. It felt like every muscle that had been tense and contracted when I was in the building just went soft. I felt relaxed for the first time in my life. And to me, no matter what the future holds, feeling that kind of peace was 100 percent worth it.

Do Something That Requires You to Face Your Losses

"Failure is just information."
—*Toni Morrison*

I did a new thing, honey.

Today I paid my taxes.

I know, I know. You might be saying, "Umm, well yeah. I hope you did, Tab!" Let me rephrase that then.

I paid my taxes . . . *early.*

Who does that?

I honestly don't know why I did it. Honey, I suppose it was one of those nudges from God again. It was two days before Christmas and during a meeting with my accountant and business manager about the upcoming tax season, I heard myself say, "You know what? Before the end of the year, let's go ahead and do this. Let's go over everything and just pay it."

First, it was a very large sum of money, so I'm so very grateful that I had it to pay. But more than anything, I'm glad I did it because it made me address some things that I didn't necessarily want to. Things that hurt me and opened up wounds that had not yet healed.

Because of legal issues, I haven't talked much about the closing of my restaurant. I'd gone into a partnership with a wonderful man, Neman, to open a second Kale My Name vegan restaurant in Los Angeles. He owned the original Chicago restaurant, and I fell in love with it while shooting *The Chi* on location. He was already looking to open another location but needed some help, and I was excited to be the one to offer just that. We opened in December 2021 and it began very well. It was such a rewarding feeling to be able to feed my community and see people gather and love on each other. Sometimes patrons would just break out in song or randomly say "Because that's my business!" They'd take selfies and group photos. We had open mic nights that were packed with both people and talent.

Unfortunately, around seven months in, we started having all kinds of problems with the building. Our ceiling started to cave in on our kitchen, and there were so many other physical issues that were making it hard to keep the place open. There was no way we would have opened the business in that building had we known up front about the preexisting issues that didn't show up in the inspection. When we complained, there was very little response. We still had hope that someone would do the right thing and fix it, so we didn't say too much about what was going on. But the most we got was a light patch up—no permanent fixes. No real repairs were done. So inevitably, because we couldn't make any headway, we had to shut down the restaurant and get legal representation to deal with the aftermath.

So today, I'm sitting with my tax accountant, seeing the true impact of the loss of the restaurant, and I'm finally able to grieve it. I'd been telling myself up until now "Oh, it will be alright—we'll be able to reopen soon," but the reality was staring me in the face. My business partner and I thought we could trust our landlord and we couldn't. We thought we could trust the building and we couldn't. We thought we had a great plan and we didn't. We thought we were doing something great for veganism, for the community, and we couldn't continue. Sitting there, staring at the numbers, I finally got a chance to sit in my loss—to process it. I was so happy when we opened. I got a chance to go and meet people from all over the world. And it all just stopped. Literally, in one day, it was all gone.

But you know what? I know God doesn't play about Tab. And honey, in the midst of all that grief, God showed me just how he planned to use even this alleged failure. My accountant turned to me and said, "Tabitha, this loss from the restaurant actually helped lower your tax bill."

"Wait a minute. The loss helped me?"

"Yes!"

Baby, ain't that a word?! As I took that information in, I realized that she was right in more ways than one. Yes, the loss of the restaurant helped me on my taxes, but it also helped me in other ways. It revealed so many things to me about people—about trust, friendship, love, and understanding. Even though it didn't succeed in the way I had hoped, it really helped me in the next chapter of my life.

It's easy to think about grief only when it comes to someone we love dying. But we grieve in other ways, too. We can grieve the loss of a friendship, a marriage, an opportunity, or, like for me, a business. Because there are myriad ways we grieve, it's so important that we take time to understand how we feel about our losses. There's no minimum or maximum time for grief. I know, I know. Some of us know how to push through it. We just keep on going because maybe our lives are such that we don't have time to deal with our feelings. But at some point, honey, you are going to have to sit with that thing.

The one thing I learned from taking the time to grieve the closing of my restaurant is, well, to make sure I always take away the lessons. Yes, we may have experienced a loss, but it doesn't have to be a total one. There are things we can take from the experience that will help us move forward. Things that, at least in business, might mean we don't lose again as we, like Aaliyah taught us, pick ourselves up and try again. Sit with what happened. Think about it. Figure out what you can take from it. Ignoring it and acting like it didn't happen will only mean that you will mess around and have the same thing happen again.

So let's address our losses and take time to process them. Even if you must push through in the immediate aftermath, don't forget to swing around again and give yourself some time when you can.

I've come to believe that grief is simply a part of every life cycle. It's part of the cycle of life in business. In friendships. In relationships. We can't always win, but we can change how we see our losses so that it ultimately ends up feeling like a win. Once you've really sat with your grief, then your next step is to come up with your game plan for moving forward. And that's when the fun begins . . . again.

Now, honey, I don't necessarily suggest you do your taxes right before Christmas, but I do hope today's new thing teaches you to embrace your losses. To take the time to process and grieve them. And to realize that sometimes, even within a loss or failure, there can be a silver lining. A nugget of something good that you can carry with you into the next venture, relationship, or whatever. Our losses are not always meant to make us feel bad. Sometimes they're meant to help us. To push us. To grow and shape us. And to absolutely teach us.

And remember that Kale My Name in Chicago is still open for business with Neman, the amazing owner and my forever friend. Please go support him. I just may see you there!

Ooh God, I thank you.

TSA
(Tabitha Service Announcement)

Losing can teach us how to win.

From Tab's "New Thing" Catalog

Host game night. Getting friends or family together for a raucous game night can also be a fun, low-stakes way to learn how to win or lose.

Create a secret handshake. Whether it's with your partner or spouse, children, nieces or nephews, having something that's just between you and someone you love can be a way to make everyone feel special.

Write a poem. Sometimes facing a loss requires that you find creative outlets for your feelings. How did that failure make you feel? How did winning that game feel in your body?

'Eat Something You've Never Eaten Before

"Just try new things. Don't be afraid.
Step out of your comfort zones and soar."
—Michelle Obama

I did a new thing.

I tried a new food.

Now anyone who knows me knows that I don't do bananas. It's something about the texture that doesn't sit right with me. I can put them in smoothies, but to just eat the raw fruit? No, thank you. But I discovered the burro banana and became curious about whether it would taste more like a regular banana or like plantains, which I absolutely love. After doing some research, I learned that these didn't taste much like bananas at all. In fact, I ended up cooking them like potatoes by sautéing them in the pan.

Honey, let me tell you! Those burro bananas were absolutely delicious. And not only that, I learned they are also good for you. They are high in iron, have anti-inflammatory properties, and are good for the eyes. Eating them encourages brain health and helps to build muscle, and they can be part of a healthy diet for people with kidney disorders. Bananas are also alkaline, which is very helpful for our immune system. I'm a firm believer that incorporating more alkaline foods into our often acidic diets is a great way to expand our options and stay healthy.

Now, what if I'd heard someone say "banana" and said, "Nah, I'm not messing with nothing called a banana!" Or I got caught up in what I thought it *might* taste like? Then I would have missed out on another healthy and delicious option to add to my pantry and incorporate into my routine.

Trying something new has a natural impact on our curiosity. When we try, say, a new food, and we love it, we're more likely to say, "I want to try something else." It gives us courage. We might even realize that we've been missing out on some great stuff because of our refusal to try something new. Now, sure, the flip side of that is sometimes you might try something new and hate it. With food, it might end up tasting totally disgusting. But honey, please don't let that turn you off to trying new things. Look at it like anything else. When you're single, you might go on dates. After going out with many people who are your "type," you might decide to try someone different. You might say, "You know what? I'm going to forget about the types. I'm just going to leave my heart and mind open and try to discover someone new." And suddenly by being open you find yourself dating someone who is completely the opposite of what you normally would go for. And maybe it turns out well. Or maybe it doesn't. But either way you learn something new about yourself. You learn a little bit more about what you like and don't like. That's the true value in trying new things.

Trying something new, even something simple like a new food, can open the door to us learning more about ourselves. Yes, something great can happen. We might find a new favorite. And yes, something not so great could happen. Many times, we don't try new things because we are afraid of that disappointment. I mean, no one *really* likes being disappointed, but some of us have a true fear of experiencing it. Well, I would encourage you to investigate that a little bit. Ask yourself why you don't like being disappointed. What comes up for you? Is this a trigger from long ago that you need to address? Be willing to figure out the source of your fear so that you can get about the business of learning something new about yourself.

I do recognize that trying something new can be a big deal for some people. For example, my sister is the pickiest eater I know. Honey, she won't even let her food touch on the same plate. She can have mac and cheese, peas, and chicken—a whole meal—but a single thing better not be touching. I didn't understand it. I would say, "Well, isn't it all going to the same place?" But that didn't matter to her. She was not having it. So imagine what it's been like all these years trying to get her to try vegan food!

That said, a wonderful thing happened recently. She came to Miami for her birthday while I was down there shooting a Target campaign with our daddy. I took them to dinner that evening, and guess what?! She ate all vegan food! Me and our daddy were just amazed, because that is not like my sister at all. But honey, she said, "You know what? I'm about to be fifty and I'm going to try something new. I know I like mushrooms, so let me see what this restaurant can do with that." And baby, she loved it! Yes, she looked at it, smelled it, and picked at it a little bit before she ate it, but she still ate it. And the next day, she had the nerve to say, "Where are we going to go to eat next?" That made me feel so good, y'all. That one leap of faith, no matter how small it might have seemed to me, made her want to try something else new. She learned that she could do it . . . and did!

Here's the thing: When we try new food, it opens our minds to something new in a very simple and basic way. If we can allow ourselves to experience a new fruit or vegetable, then we are teaching ourselves to be curious about other new things. And maybe when we do that, we find out that there is much more to learn about ourselves, and so much more good in the world to discover.

TSA
(Tabitha Service Announcement)

It's the simple leaps of faith that reveal the most.

From Tab's "New Thing" Catalog

Try a new fruit. Maybe you're the type of person who can put away some protein and loves vegetables, but your fruit intake is low. Find a couple of fruit options you love and try swapping them in the next time you want sugar or candy.

Try a new veggie. Vegetables have so many health benefits, but it's still hard for some people to eat them regularly. Decide to try a new veggie every few days until you find one you love, or at least can eat more often.

Try a dairy alternative. In under a decade, we've been given so many more nondairy options for food and drinks. Try some oat milk in your cereal this week, or a vegan ice cream flavor you've never tried before.

Meet My Play Cousin…
Mae Did a New Thing

In my junior year of college, a sushi bar opened down the street from campus. I'll never forget that. We all knew about the restaurant because they'd begun to leave coupons and menus in the lobby of our dorm. They also ran discounted specials for college students—things like $2 sushi rolls and happy hour drinks that appealed to older students on campus. Everyone on my floor in the dorm raved about this place. They went on and on about the shrimp tempura and the wide variety of sushi they had. But I was not interested at all. I did not do raw fish.

Yes, they told me I could try cooked fish options or California rolls, but it didn't make sense to me. If you're going to a sushi bar and sushi is raw fish, then, obviously, you should be eating raw fish. But since I didn't like raw fish, I wouldn't go to the sushi bar.

This happened every weekend. Every Friday after classes, my roommate would try to drag me out, and the first thing I asked is "Where are we going?" If it was the ten-cent wing spot or the vegan place around the corner, I was down. But if she said the sushi bar? "No, thank you." I stayed in and got plenty of studying done or blasted through my nights and weekends on my cell phone talking with my boyfriend, who went to college the next state over.

Fast-forward to today, I'm still not a fan of sushi. Or at least I thought I wasn't—until a couple of weeks ago when a girlfriend of mine who I hadn't seen in forever invited me out to lunch. She called me and gave me the address, but I didn't recognize the location. It didn't even occur to me to ask about the restaurant, because I don't eat sushi and so it's never ever on my radar. I just said I would meet her at the address. Even when I plugged it into my GPS, nothing familiar popped up. So when I pulled up to meet her for lunch, and realized it was a sushi bar, I was devastated.

Why didn't I like it? I don't know. I think it was just the idea of raw fish. All I could see in my mind was the fish my dad brought home from his fishing expeditions with my uncles. I remember the fish eyeballs and their wide-open mouths in the sink as he cut, gutted, and filleted them. This was all in preparation for my mother to fry them up for fish sandwiches. So the idea that I would be eating what I saw in the sink before it ever got any flour or seasoning or oil just turned my stomach.

What was I going to do? I was there. My friend was waving me over to her table. And I really wanted to spend time with her. Again, we hadn't seen each other in a long time. But I absolutely did not want to eat any sushi. When I got to the table, we hugged and talked a bit before the waiter came over to take our order.

My friend ordered her food and then just looked at me. And I looked back at her. Then I had what can only be described as a light bulb moment. I thought, *You are really thinking about cutting this visit short—and for what? What exactly are you going to sacrifice this time with someone you care about for? Fear? Is this idea of something that you think you don't like worth missing this opportunity for connection?* So I did it. I did a new thing.

I asked my friend what she would suggest, and like many people, "Do you like raw or cooked?" Again, I had the same thought as decades before. Why go to a sushi bar and not actually have raw sushi?

"You know what? I'll try raw."

She just looked at me. She remembered.

"Okay."

She ordered me something that I have no idea how to pronounce, and when it arrived, I looked down and was suddenly, deeply concerned. Of course, it didn't look like the fish that my dad brought home from his fishing trips, but it was still raw fish wrapped neatly in rice. I wasn't sure if I could eat it. I tried to stall by talking and catching up a little bit more but then she, being my friend from way back, caught on and said, "Try it."

"Okay."

I picked up the first roll and dipped it into some soy sauce before quickly putting it in my mouth. I chewed and chewed and chewed.

It wasn't that bad.

It wasn't the best thing I'd ever tasted in the world, but it wasn't bad at all. As I thought more about it later when I got home, I realized that it wasn't terrible that I'd missed out on all those opportunities to hang out with friends on weekends back in college. But I came to understand that one has to be ready to do a new thing. Clearly, I wasn't ready back then, and maybe I was only barely ready now. I'm grateful for the recognition that trying new things is wonderful, and it's also okay not to be terribly impressed by the new thing. I don't have to beat myself up about it, but I'm glad I at least tried.

Now, will I be running off to try more sushi? Probably not. But if a good friend who I love and care about invites me out to lunch at a sushi bar, I most definitely won't allow fear to make me say no.

Wear Something Out of Your Norm

"You all can judge my body all you want,
but at the end of the day it's my body.
I love it and I'm comfortable in my own skin."
—*Simone Biles*

I did a new thing.

I wore a fitted dress.

Now listen, y'all know that when you see Tab, I usually have on something colorful and comfortable. Whether that's an avocado jogging suit or a multipatterned, A-line dress with fun, platform high-top sneakers, I intentionally choose cute and comfort over sexy and fitted. I also rarely wear all red. I will put on some pink or blue or even bright green but red is not a go-to color for me. But recently, as I've begun to do these new things, I had to stop and ask myself, "Why, Tab?" Why don't I wear fitted dresses?

Why don't I wear red? And that's when it came to me: I don't wear these things because I feel like it brings too much attention to my body.

And, Tab?

I know, I know. I had to dig into that thang a bit further, too. There is certainly a part of me that doesn't want to show too much of my body because I want to save that for my husband. These curves are for his eyes only. But honestly, there is also a part of me that is still becoming comfortable with being bigger than I used to be. Yes, I'm free, but every healing journey is a process. And I realized today that I'm still processing what it means to be this size in a business and industry that idolizes disordered eating and conforming to certain smaller sizes. The old Tab would freak out if my weight climbed above 140 or I was bigger than a size four. I used to wear fitted stuff all the time to look "the part." To put out an image that was pretty far away from who I really was. It's the same reason I straightened my hair and hid my Southern accent for years.

So when I first started gaining weight—I'm about twenty-five pounds heavier than I used to be—I didn't like it. I'd been conditioned by Hollywood to believe that my success depended on me being "the perfect size." As a result, I did all kinds of two-a-day workouts and starvation diets. But honey, we all know now that standard wasn't true, right? My success was never dependent on what size I wore. And yet still, at the beginning of my freedom walk, I started wearing loose-fitting clothes in order to make myself feel smaller. I wasn't yet secure enough with my extra curves, despite being the healthiest I'd been in a really long time.

But honey, tonight I threw those insecurities in the trash. I stepped out to my birthday dinner in a fitted red dress and felt wonderful. It was still comfortable like I like it, but it definitely hugged every one of these curves.

"Oh, babe, I like this. You don't wear stuff like this no more," my husband said.

"Girl, you have lost a lot of weight," all my friends said.

I hadn't, though. I rarely wore anything fitted, so it only appeared like I lost weight because they always see me in loose clothes. But baby, I had so much fun in my red dress. It not only made me feel happy, I felt sexy. Now I'm thinking I might buy more fitted clothing.

Isn't that what always happens when we try something new? It opens us up to thinking about things we might have missed out on. Tab loves fashion and there are probably thousands of cute outfits I've been passing up. No more!

I must say, I'm proud of myself. I looked in the mirror, and before letting doubt and insecurity take hold, I said to myself, "Wait a minute, Tab. Girl, you can wear whatever you want. Embrace those curves. So what if somebody sees them? That's why they're there. Not just necessarily for Chance, but also for me to love myself and to appreciate this body that I'm in."

It's such a freeing thing to step outside of my comfort zone and wear something more body conscious. It gives me even more confidence. In this new season of my life, I'm constantly reminding myself that I can have whatever body I have, in whatever size or shape, and it's absolutely beautiful. I can also have my dreams with this body! It's mine. I'm happy. My husband loves it. And that's that.

Now don't get me wrong, I still really enjoy loose-fitting clothes. And I still don't like all the attention the tighter clothes bring. But honey, if I feel like it, I will wear my fitted red dress and embrace the moment and attention! I'm allowed to change my mind, and that's my business.

And guess what? You can, too.

Maybe your issue is not with fitted clothes. Maybe you want to try wearing sneakers instead of high heels. Or maybe you want to try those jeans in the back of your closet that you never wear because you are worried about them beautiful hips of yours. So many women learn very early on how to hide our perceived imperfections. We find ways to play down the parts of our bodies we feel insecure about. If you have hips, thighs, and fries like I do, then like me, you probably know how to accentuate your waist and make it so that you look smaller than you are. And honestly, I don't think anything is wrong with that. As I always say, do what makes you feel good. At the same time, don't feel locked in to dressing one way. If you're putting off wearing something, put it off no further. Embrace that insecurity and allow yourself to live a little. You have every right to change your mind. It's true freedom to be willing to give yourself options.

TSA
(Tabitha Service Announcement)

*Living life your way is the freedom
we all deserve!*

From Tab's "New Thing" Catalog

Get dressed up just because. Honey, I'm talking about getting glammed up to go to the mall or post office. Yes, put on that fancy dress to go get some gas. It's so much fun to watch how people react to you, and I guarantee you'll feel good about yourself.

Make a "get dressed" playlist. I know many people who love to have a soundtrack for when they are getting dressed. Some people play all hip-hop, others prefer smooth jazz. Create your playlist and include music that will you get excited about getting dressed for your day or night.

Throw your family or friends a tea party. Here's another reason to get dressed up. Throw on your gloves and fancy hat—or not, that's your business—and invite your people for a special tea party.

Do Something (or Nothing) with Your Hair

"When I cut my hair, the whole sound changed, my style changed."
—*Rihanna*

I did a new thing.

I changed my hair.

It may seem like a small thing, but with God, it's never a small thing. Underneath every move I'm compelled to make, there's always a lesson or purpose. I am in Miami this weekend, and yesterday, at my photoshoot, I decided to switch things up a bit with my hair. Now, y'all know Donna always has something to say when I take her out of her natural state, my afro. But I told her to hush, because this is something I've been wanting to do for a while and she was going to be just fine.

"I just turned forty-four. Do you think I could do two little Minnie Mouse ponytails? The kind that are like Princess Leia balls?" I asked my hairstylist.

She got so excited! I'd never worn my hair that way, and she loves it when I stretch my limits and do something new with Donna. "Oh yes, girl, let's do it! Let's do it!"

So she parted and pinned my hair until we had two of the cutest balls on each side of my head, with the back hanging down in twists. Listen, honey, you couldn't tell me or Donna a single thing. We got so many compliments that day. People were loving it, and more than that, I loved it. I felt so cute, so young. It was like the shift in my hairstyle shifted something in my spirit, too. It took me back to those days of being a preteen and just skipping along, minding my young business. The joy of that feeling had me smiling all day.

So today I had an event that included a bunch of children, and when I sat in the hair and makeup chair, I decided that I wanted to keep that youthful spirit present.

"You know what?" I said. "This time, girl, let's do two balls again but don't leave any hair down in the back."

And of course, she was on it.

Honey, when those kids saw me and Donna, their eyes just lit up. It made me so happy to see their eyes widen. Nearly every single child said, "Miss Tab, I loooove your hair!"

I truly thought I was going to bust on the inside. The simple decision to do something new with my hair made me feel like I was one of them. Like a kid again.

For so many of us, our hair is part of our identity. So trying a new hairstyle can sometimes demonstrate a powerful movement toward change in other areas of our lives. I'm thinking about the woman who does a big chop. When I did my first big chop, I remember feeling overwhelmed with this strange new confidence. I kept saying, "Ooh, I can see my face. I love my face this way." But maybe it's not about a big chop for you. Maybe you always change your hair and now you want to leave it alone and let it grow out. Maybe you're the sister who decides to move from relaxed hair to locs (or vice versa). Maybe you want to cut you some bangs or pull your hair back off your face for a change. Honey, the woman who changes her hair is on a mission. Nine times out of ten, she is in the middle of a changing season in her life, too. Not to mention that changing our hair really does have the power to change our mood and energy. There have been so many times when I've changed Donna and end up feeling like a completely different person. And, men, that includes you, too! You can switch up as well, honey, because finding new things is your business also.

Deeper than that, though, a new hairstyle—maybe even more so than a new outfit, lipstick, or shoes—can change the direction of where we're going in life. It definitely changes how we feel. We show up differently. That alone is why I think doing something different with your hair can be worth any anxiety we might feel in the moment about doing it.

And get this: sometimes when we change our hair, it changes

our mind. The way we think. We can finally see clearly and begin to show up in spaces differently. At the same time, our hair will sometimes change how some people treat us. I've seen this for myself. When I wear my afro, the respect I get is completely different from how I'm received when I wear my hair in long braids or when I used to wear it straight. I think some of it is generational. When I wear my fro, elders, especially within the Black community, will give me this proud smile. It's like they are secretly thinking "Yes, sister" as I'm reminding them of days gone by.

Of course, there will also be people who won't understand your change. I sometimes get nasty looks from people who aren't ready to embrace the free part of themselves, or who take issue with me wearing my afro so proudly. I never take their looks or comments personally, though, because I know their issue isn't with me. Their problem lies within. They just choose to project their own lack of self-esteem or beliefs about what's respectable or not on me.

But honey, that ain't my business. I know the power hair holds. I know it tells a story. And all me and Donna can do is keep telling mine.

TSA
(Tabitha Service Announcement)

*We may not want change, but sometimes
change is needed to make our lives the better.*

From Tab's "New Thing" Catalog

Try a new hairstyle. If you've always worn your hair straight, maybe try it curly this week. And vice versa—if you're a curly girl, maybe try it straight. Love a ponytail? Go 'head and let it all hang loose.

Get some braids or add some extensions. I love it when I put Donna in braids for a braidcation. It not only gives her a rest, it feels good to see my hair in a different style from what I'm used to.

Dye your hair a new color—or let your gray come on in. Sometimes we need more than a cute new hairstyle. Consider trying a dramatic change in color or, if you always color your hair, think about wearing your hair in its natural hue for a while.

Meet My Play Cousin...
Kayla Did a New Thing

I started growing my locs about ten years ago when I graduated from high school. It was something I knew I wanted to do even before the whole YouTube/IG hair vloggers started posting tips on how to care for them. My first twists were started right before I began college, and I've been growing them ever since. They easily reached my tailbone at one point.

I recently finished graduate school and decided to move to the West Coast from Baltimore, where I grew up and went to school. I've been wanting to work in the tech field in Silicon Valley for such a long time so when an awesome, well-paying opportunity came my way, I jumped at it. And now I'm thinking about my locs and wondering if I want to take another big step in my life. But even as I accepted the position, I knew that it wouldn't be the only big move I'd make. It was time to cut my locs.

When I started growing them, I was so determined that I would never cut them off. I loved the way I looked in them, and they became such a part of my identity. I was the woman with the locs that worked as a work-study student in financial aid. I was the Black girl with locs in the engineering department. People knew me by my hair. And maybe that's just it. It was time for people to know me by something else.

I know some people don't believe that there's power and energy in one's hair, but I do, especially as a Black woman who's always having her hair critiqued. Because of that, I believe that changing my hair can also shift that energy. Change is good. Whether I am changing jobs, addresses, or my hair, being willing to do something new can change how you feel on the inside. I'm a witness.

Making small changes to your physical appearance can have a big impact, so imagine what this big change would do. I went to the shop yesterday and held each loc in my hand as the barber cut it. I went from almost butt-length hair to having less than a half inch on top of my head. And I feel amazing!

There's something so freeing about this experience. I can feel the breeze as it moves through my tiny afro. When I take my hand and run it along the back of my head where it's cut the closest, I no longer feel the weight. The weight of the actual locs that used to be there, yes, but also the weight of my life on the East Coast. It wasn't a bad life. At all. But it was the life I had as a child and college student. And now I want a different life—one that symbolizes my adulthood. This big chop is the beginning for me. I look forward to seeing all the blessings that come on the other side of me doing this new thing.

DAY 16

Create a New Memory with Your Family

"The most beautiful things are not associated with money; they are memories and moments. If you don't celebrate those, they can pass you by."
—*Alek Wek*

I did a new thing.

On Christmas Day, my husband and I surprised our son, Quest, with tickets to watch and meet his favorite NBA player, Damian Lillard, in Portland, Oregon. A month prior we'd surprised him with a video call from Damian and, honey, our baby boy cried so hard. We knew then that we had to do one better for Christmas.

I suppose we could have waited until the Trailblazers played in L.A., but we thought it would be great to do a whole surprise flight to Portland to watch Damian play at home. And listen, if you've ever kept a secret from your children or surprised them in any way, then I know you know the joy that fills your heart when they finally figure out what's going on. That morning as we opened presents, we handed him a card and told him to read it aloud. As he read the following words—*You are going to Portland to see Dame play!*—his voice began to shake and he took off running. My baby boy jumped up and down, then ran straight into my arms for the biggest hug. He was so full of emotion, honey, that tears ran down his face. He gave me the sweetest "Thank you!" I felt like I won the lottery when I saw his reaction. We all cried tears of happiness together. The surprise was again a success.

And that's just it, right? When we do something special for someone else, yes, we're doing it for them, but the spillover is that it will also bring us joy. We get to share in their happiness. I love to bless people and try to do it often, but I'd never done something like this before—something so big and spontaneous—and now I want to lean into giving even more.

Quest's surprise trip wasn't set for way off in the future. We were leaving the very next day. The day after Christmas we got on a plane and flew to Portland. It was our entire family's first time there, and I was so excited because I'd heard there were plenty of vegan options, and that was going to be needed because we had to be back in Los Angeles in—wait for it—twenty-four hours. The last thing I wanted was to have to search high and low for food I could actually eat. And yes, we were literally going to Portland for one day only.

Now, honey, I honestly wasn't sure about that at first. I kept trying to figure out how to make it work so we could stay longer. I thought it would be such a waste of money to just fly in for one day.

But eventually, my husband and I decided that we were just going to make it happen. We can do something new this time. It was our baby boy, after all. We could do it for him! We decided to fly out in the morning, go to the game in the evening, and come back home the next morning.

And we did it! It was perfect!

As soon as we landed, we got a car and went straight to the hotel, where we grabbed some food. Tab was hungry, y'all. Then we relaxed a bit before freshening up and getting ready to go to the game. It was a little rushed, but when I saw the way Quest's eyes lit up when we arrived at the Moda Center and he got the chance to finally meet Damian in person, I knew it was worth it. Honey, sometimes it ain't about the length of a trip—it's more about the intention of the trip. That's what makes a getaway worthwhile. We set an intention to do this thing for our child, did what we needed to do to make that thang happen. And the fruit of it all was the big smile I see in all the pictures Quest took with Damian and at courtside, and the joy that fills my heart thinking about the memories we made.

That's what this new thing was really about for me. In twenty-four hours, we were able to create a family memory that will last a lifetime. To this day, Quest talks about that trip. If I even mention Damian, it's like he's back on cloud nine. He'll never forget it, and neither will I.

I encourage you to do something new by going to a place you've never gone before and creating a new memory for yourself, a friend, or a family member. No, it doesn't have to be an overnight NBA game. It could be picking up your baby from school for a late lunch or early dinner. It could be a staycation with your mom where you hang out at the hotel's indoor pool all day. Whatever it is, don't hold yourself hostage or forgo making wonderful memories because you think you don't have enough time or money. You might need only one day.

Unfortunately, too many of us don't realize the importance of creating memories until we've lost a loved one. I was blessed to have a mother who understood the significance of creating family memories. As a little girl, we were always going on local trips, and she would always say, "These will be our memories one day." And my daddy loved capturing our moments. He was always the one with the camera taking a bunch of pictures and video.

On the other hand, my husband's experience was very different. He didn't have any of that. There were no trips as a kid, and there was no one taking pictures. He has barely any pictures of himself as a little boy, and it's something that really hurts him now. There are times when he wishes he had taken pictures with his great-grandmother, especially since she's passed on.

And that's really the heart of what I think God was saying to me today. The unfortunate truth is that one day memories will be the only thing we have left. We don't live forever in this body but we do in the hearts and minds of our loved ones. Honey, making and capturing these memories will make us smile so much when the people in those pictures aren't here with us anymore. It's the memories that we can hold and cherish forever. It's the memories that help us keep our joy and laughter. It's the memories that drive those old stories we end up telling at the barbecue or family reunion.

All I have left of my mama is memories. All I have left of my grandparents is memories. So with my own family, I want to create as many as I can.

To be clear, I don't mean we should rush things in order to create memories. I don't mean manufacturing moments. I just mean being present and soaking up an experience. Yes, capture it, but also be sure to really take it in. There are ten years between my children, Choyce and Quest. I remember being so young when I had Choyce and saying things like "I can't wait until she's this or that age." But honey, she's grown now, and while I love the woman she's becoming, I miss my baby girl. With Quest, well, Tab has learned some things. I want him to be my little boy for as long as possible, because the reality is, our children are only children for a very short amount of time. We get a good twelve years of them being our babies, and then the teen years hit and before you know it they are eighteen and technically adults for the rest of our lives. I want to make all the memories with him while I can, but I'm not going to rush them. I'm no longer saying, "I can't wait until he's this or that age." I'm taking it one day at a time, one basketball game at a time, one grateful smile at a time.

TSA
(Tabitha Service Announcement)

Time is on your side if you use it wisely.

From Tab's "New Thing" Catalog

Find an alternative to traveling with family. Maybe you don't have family or friends you can travel with. That's okay—here is something else you can do. When you are away, send a postcard to a family member. This is a small but great way to share the experience with your family and friends.

Explore your own city. Every city and state has some interesting historical background. Maybe take a tour within your own town. Learn something new about where you live. That will give you an opportunity to share your something new with others in your city or visitors.

Volunteer at one of the local charities. Sometimes your "something new" will be a thing that allows you to give of your time and energy to those who are in need. By serving people and communities in this way, you will inevitably see your own personal growth.

Explore
New Ways to
Communicate

"Great communication begins with connection."
—*Oprah Winfrey*

I did a new thing.

I began learning American Sign Language (ASL) to communicate with a deaf actor on the set of *Tab Time*.

Troy Kotsur is an Oscar-winning deaf actor who visited the show as a guest. He's also an amazing human being. This was the first time I'd ever worked with someone who communicates only via sign language, and I'm so grateful to him for his patience with me. In addition to learning how to use my hands to sign, I also discovered just how important our nonverbals are to our being able to speak to each other. I pointed and picked up things, and honey,

I used my eyes and my whole body to have wonderful conversations with Troy. By the end of the day, it felt like I'd been with an old friend the whole time.

I can admit that learning the signs I did today was challenging for me, because more than anything I wanted to make sure I wasn't doing anything offensive. Getting it exactly right was so important. I wanted to refrain from doing anything that would appear like I was cutting corners. I kept saying to myself, "Tab, girl, you better get this right." Little children and parents all around the world, some who are deaf or hard of hearing, were going to be watching and I wanted to do right by them. Gratefully, once I realized that not only were Troy and I communicating using ASL but we were also communicating in the language of love, I was able to relax and trust him and the interpreter we had on set.

Spending the day with Troy took me back to my childhood when I would spend time with my great-great-aunt Bett. She was also deaf but did not know ASL. There was no one in our small town who could teach it to her. As a child, though, I was so drawn to her and knew how to communicate with her. Aunt Bett and our family created our own way of speaking that wasn't ASL, and what I've come to realize is that children are not as hung up on things as adults are. We can learn something from the way they approach life. I was able to communicate with Aunt Bett because I didn't realize she was deaf. I just thought she communicated differently and did what I needed to in order to talk to her. Children don't care if they speak the same language as someone else as long as love and kindness are present. I think that's what I understood about my aunt Bett. She didn't have ASL, but she had a deep love that helped her "hear" us, and us, her.

Love just kind of overpowers everything, doesn't it? Laughter and joy, too. And that was the same with Troy on set. Yes, it's *Tab Time,* so there was lots of play and fun. But there was also lots of love and kindness to fill any perceived gaps.

Honey, this new thing has awakened something inside of Tab. My desire to get this just right didn't come out of nowhere. God was using it. When we are doing something new that will affect other people, we have to be mindful that we aren't, as the elders used to say, doing things "any ol' kind of way." We have to respect them as much as we want to be respected. This episode on American Sign Language wasn't just about me experiencing something new. It was about showing representation and inclusion in a positive way.

And without a doubt, there needs to be more representation of deaf people on our big and small screens. My experience today has inspired me to one day take some classes or watch some videos to learn ASL myself. I've also been talking with my fellow producers about what it might look like to have an interpreter for every episode. The thing is, none of this would have come to mind had I not opened myself up to doing something new on the show.

Representation and accessibility matters. I remember when my mama was sick. She became paralyzed and limited to a bed or wheelchair due to ALS. Whenever I'd fly back and forth from L.A. to North Carolina to visit her, I would look at those tiny bathrooms and wonder how anyone who was in a wheelchair would be able to go if they needed to. I remember asking a flight attendant that very thing. "Oh, I don't know. No one's ever asked," she said. I was shocked. And every time I asked that, I'd get some version of the same response. A shrug and an "I don't know." That breaks my heart. And maybe back then, my questions didn't mean much to those airlines, but now that my voice might carry a little weight, I really want to bring awareness to this issue that is negatively affecting the differently abled. They deserve to be able to fly comfortably. But first, I'll start where I can. How can *Tab Time* improve the experience of the viewers who are deaf and hard of hearing?

As you might have figured out by now, doing a new thing has a ripple effect. You might think you're doing it for yourself, and honey, yes to that! But usually God will use your curiosity and open heart to not only help you get free but to sometimes help other people. As I said, I wasn't contemplating learning ASL before Troy's visit. Maybe I should have been, but it wasn't something that I felt I needed before. But engaging with him opened my heart and mind to the possibilities of not only how I might build relationships with the deaf community for myself, but also how I might influence others to do the same.

Listen, we are all in this world together, and we have got to figure out how to communicate with each other and love on each other no matter what we look like or how we happen to show up. We must take the time to help each other take up space. I'm excited that I've found one more way I can do just that.

TSA
(Tabitha Service Announcement)

*Depending on how you use it,
communication can unlock so much
goodness in our lives.*

From Tab's "New Thing" Catalog

Play a game of charades. Not only is this a good time, but it's the kind of game that will help you learn how to communicate differently. Our nonverbal communication is just as important as the verbal so why not explore that while having some fun?

Color in a coloring book. There are all kinds of adult coloring books that will help you focus and calm down when things might be hectic. Honey, coloring can be so soothing, and your inner child will be so happy for a chance to express themselves.

Look through an old photo album. I know we are used to having a million digital photos on our phones nowadays, but looking through old photos will bring back amazing memories and spark conversation with family and friends.

Do Something That Intimidates You

"How we handle our fears will determine where we go with the rest of our lives. To experience adventure or to be limited by the fear of it."
—Judy Blume

I did a new thing.

Baby, today I made my own vegan Caesar salad dressing for the first time.

Really, Tab? That's it?

I know y'all might not think that's a big deal, because I'm always trying things in the kitchen. Many times with great success, but sometimes not so much—and that's my business. (We won't discuss the Jamaican ackee mishap of 2020; they still welcomed me in Jamaica, though.) But I've been avoiding making Caesar salad dressing for a good long time. First off, there's only a handful of vegan restaurants who really know how to make a tasty Caesar. One is a full five-hour flight away in New York. The other place is in L.A., but I just learned they use soy in the base, which gives me severe headaches. Nope, can't do that anymore! So if I wanted a good dressing, it looked like the only real solution was to make my own. But honey, I had really convinced myself I couldn't do it. I've been telling myself for years: "Tab, you can't make no Caesar dressing! You won't be able to get the flavor right."

Well, that stopped today.

Let me tell you, I got in my kitchen and said a prayer. I said, "Lord, you're going to guide me through this and I'm trusting you to make it right." Then Tab got into it. In the past, I'd always first thought about the nonvegan version of any recipe I was working with and tried to figure out how to substitute what I could. Well, if it ain't broke, don't fix it, right? I looked up what makes regular Caesar dressing great and decided to veganize what I could. Eggs were easy to switch out. So was the mayo. But I was shocked to learn that anchovies were one of the main ingredients in the most delicious versions of the dressing. Good thing I had a replacement for that, too. Once I figured out all I needed, Tab got to work, y'all.

Baby, let me tell you!

No, this ain't no cookbook, honey, but y'all finna get this recipe for Tab's Caesar dressing. I first mixed up some vegan mayo, lemon juice, and a chopped garlic clove. Then I added some garlic powder. A little or a lot, that's your business. Next came a splash of liquid coconut aminos, along with a good amount of Kelly's Crouton

Lemon Pepper Parmesan. But honey, if you have nutritional yeast, you can absolutely use that instead. Then I added a pinch of salt and pepper and some chopped capers and topped all that off with some freshly chopped garlic. Honey, I stirred it up like so, and when I licked the knife—yes, I used a butter knife to mix it because that's my business—all I could say was "My God, My God!" It was like a little light that I didn't even realize was missing had returned, y'all. I was so proud of myself, I took off running in the house. I took my kale, cut up some cucumbers—no, they don't go in Caesar salad but *again,* that's my business—and drenched it all in my homemade dressing.

I still can't believe it. I just made a Caesar salad dressing that I absolutely love. And yes, that's a big deal.

I'm always amazed at how something so simple can put you in the best of moods. I'd missed a good Caesar. I realized it was tied to so many amazing memories for me. My husband and I used to go to dinner every Friday to a restaurant in Greensboro, North Carolina, called Oh Brian's. We would always order the Caesar salad and then talk about how much we loved it. It never got old! Over the years in Los Angeles we'd try to find similar-tasting dressings, but the store-bought ones, especially the vegan versions, never hit right. This is why I fought through my resistance and finally made the dressing myself, and it was truly the highlight of the day.

There are two types of resistances that will show up in your mind and body when you are thinking about trying something new. Sometimes there's a healthy resistance. This is usually a sign that we need to take our time and process what we're about to do before moving forward with it. There might be many factors and considerations we need to make before taking the leap. But what we experience most of the time is what I call toxic resistance. This is usually a kind of internal pushback that comes because we have talked ourselves out of doing that thing. You'll know your resistance is toxic when there's literally no other reason to not do that new thing except that you are scared. When fear is the only obstacle, it's generally a sign that we need to move forward. Yes, we still might be afraid, but don't give fear the power to stop you from trying something that just might have your blessing on the other side of it.

Tab, I thought we were just talking about salad dressing?!

Listen, honey, resistance will come for the big and the small things. In high school, I was afraid of taking a drama class because everybody told me the teacher was mean and terrible. So what did young Tab do? Baby, I put it off. In my senior year, when I finally got the nerve to take the class, I realized that it was absolutely amazing. I lost the opportunity to study under this awesome teacher for all four years because (1) I was listening to what other people said, and (2) I was scared. If the only thing stopping you from doing your new thing today—whether it's making a salad dressing or leaving a bad relationship—is fear, then I want you to push through that resistance. Don't feed into it. No, that fear's probably not going anywhere, and you might have to process your feelings around it. Maybe figure out what kind of fear it is. Is it fear of the unknown? Fear of failure? Fear of success? But once you've sat with it for a while, make your move, honey. Get on with it! I'm a witness that pressing through that toxic resistance will often lead to you feeling amazing and/or experiencing something beyond your wildest imagination.

Today's new thing also made me think about how many times we convince ourselves we can't do something and then, when we actually do it, we realize just how much time we wasted with those thoughts. We see how much greatness we missed out on because we were afraid. Doesn't it make you want to kick yourself when you've talked crazy to yourself about something for a million years, and when you finally break down and do it, you master that thing on the first try? Let's stop that, alright? You're doubting yourself when you could just be out here being amazing. Even me, the one who is always trying new things. Writing a whole book about it. I let Caesar dressing intimidate me. But that's okay. Healing is a process. Now . . . who wants a salad?

TSA
(Tabitha Service Announcement)

*Don't feed the resistance caused by fear.
Push through it. There's a blessing
on the other side.*

From Tab's "New Thing" Catalog

Try an adventurous sport or activity. My husband, Chance, is working through his new thing list and there are two things he wants to try: surfing and skiing. So why not try something like that yourself? Both surfing and skiing bring you closer to nature, whether it's the power of the ocean or the mountain.

Plan a trip. This might seem like an easy one, but I'm always surprised by people who are intimidated by travel. They say, "How do I know what to plan or what to do or where to go?" But guess what? You'll figure it out. And maybe, just maybe, you'll have fun doing it.

Go camping. And honey, you don't even have to go way out into the woods somewhere to do this. Wouldn't it be fun to set up a tent in your backyard? Get some family and friends together, start a fire, and roast some hot dogs—vegan, of course—and enjoy the outdoors.

Meet My Play Cousin…
Leslie Did a New Thing

My favorite television shows are all on HGTV. As a matter of fact, I am a DIY and HGTV fanatic. I love the idea that people can go into a space, a house, and transform it into something beautiful—into someone's sanctuary. And I wanted that for myself. Every day I walked from our garage through our laundry room to get to the rest of our house. And every day I was disgusted by the peeling paint on the walls, the old shelving, and the tile floors that were chipped and missing. We just purchased our home a year ago and have been slowly making our way through various renovations we've needed. We gutted and remodeled the kitchen and refreshed the guest bathroom. However, most of those renovations required a contractor who would come in and handle the electrical or plumbing, so I thought that would be the same with the laundry room.

But then I got a notion. It was time for me to do a new thing. I was going to renovate the laundry room myself with a little help from my husband. I was scared a little bit. Actually, I was scared a lot of bit. I'd never done anything like that before. Yes, I've done some refinishing of furniture and painting walls, but this was another beast. Pulling up floors and installing sinks was a whole other ballgame. But I was willing to give it a try. My incentive for doing so was that I was finally going to be able to do exactly what I wanted in the space. I could make it look exactly the way I wanted.

So I got to work.

We pulled up the floors and my husband helped me lay down the dark-colored engineered hardwood that I wanted. I was able to take the existing shelves and sand them down, refinish, and paint them. I went with a sleek black-and-white motif for the design, and I even created a cat corner for our precious kitty so she could have her own space for the kitty litter.

When all was said and done and I did my final reveal to family and friends, I broke down in tears. I did it! I had such an overwhelming feeling of accomplishment because I was able to accomplish something I never thought I'd be able to do without significant outside help.

Of course I educated myself by scrolling through YouTube University and watching how various people did their DIY projects. I was careful to take a cue from their mistakes to ensure that I didn't repeat them. And while the laundry room is certainly not perfect, it's way more functional and beautiful than it ever was before. I'm so proud of myself! And you know, to my husband's chagrin, I'm looking around the house to see what other projects I could take on next. Especially since I know all those years of watching HGTV and reading the DIY magazines have paid off.

Maybe hubby will let me get to work on his man cave.

Do a New Thing That's Really an Old, Old Thing

"Be willing to be a beginner every single morning."
—*Meister Eckhart*

I did a new thing.

I started playing the flute today.

Well, almost.

Remember that private school we were considering for Quest? Well, today was the parents' interview. After a brief introduction we were given another private tour, this time of active classrooms while school was in session. Of course I was still in awe of everything we were seeing. It was hard not to think about how different my life would have been if I had had access to some of those programs when I was in school. On the tour, we learned that there are two parts of the curriculum that's required for incoming sixth graders. First, all students are required to take at least one year of Latin beginning in sixth grade. Second, they are all required to take a music class in which they learn to play the violin.

Honey, my mind was blown! I sat in one room and watched a group of eleven- and twelve-year-olds, from every race and ethnicity you can imagine, playing the violin and learning to read music. The tears were ready to drop, y'all. I got so emotional thinking, *Wow, if everyone had access to these kinds of resources, if everyone was exposed to new things at this age, what would that do to our brains? How great would that be for our world? How much more of our potential would we all reach?*

I also began to think about the benefits Quest would gain if he learned an instrument. There's so much research out there that links musical ability with improvement in other academic subjects, like math and science. And that's when it hit me! I wanted to take that journey with him. If Quest gets into the school and starts playing the violin, then I will take up an instrument with him. I will do a new thing, too!

Except it's not exactly a new thing.

I started playing in the band in the seventh grade and continued through my sophomore year of high school. Honey, Tab played that flute, and I was good, too! I never got first chair, but I was always in the running. The closest I got was the third chair, but even then, I still knew that I had great potential. I truly enjoyed playing the flute.

However, by the time I got to the tenth grade, my interests had expanded. I'd started playing on the basketball team and was juggling both the band and ball before I put them both down when I was in my car accident. I injured my neck in the accident, and everything changed for me after that. I decided I was going to be a hippie, a woman who was "one with the land," and, as a result, I believed that there was no room in my life for all those extracurriculars. I truly thought that if I was going to be this carefree hippie then I could not focus on things like playing the flute or playing basketball. I thought I had to make a choice.

Honey, hindsight is 20/20, as they say. I now know I didn't have to choose. Yes, I had to give up basketball because of my injury, but I could have continued to play the flute. And nothing is stopping me from picking it up again now.

"Let's go to the music store," I said to my husband as we left the school.

Stepping inside the store brought back all the sweet memories of being in the band in high school. My mind went right back to those days. It felt like I was in eighth grade again. Walking into the band room back then, there were always chairs lined in a half circle with rows of them on each riser. Being in the music store literally took me back, honey! I remembered trying to play nineties R&B music, which was nothing like what was actually on our sheet music.

I snapped out of my trip down memory lane when my husband looked at me and said, "Look at you smiling all hard!" He was right. I had reverted back to being a teenage band member! I immediately asked the sales associate if they could help me with a flute. He apologized and told me they didn't have them in stock. If they had, Tab would have left that store with a flute in her hand. But I'm going to place my order online, and really soon I'm going to get back to playing again. For now—at least until this book is published—I think I will keep my new hobby a secret. Something special, just for me. And then when I'm ready to share with my internet family, I will. But no matter when that happens, I'm so excited about doing *this* old-but-new-again thing.

Sometimes your new thing is actually an old thing you left behind long ago. An old hobby or talent that you were once passionate about but lost in the ups and downs of life. Why don't you try to pick it back up again? Baby, I get it. Life happens and it's easy to get distracted. I loved playing the flute but I let it go, too. As an adult, you often forget the things that you may have enjoyed as a child or as a young adult. Maybe you thought you couldn't do it alongside other activities that took priority. Maybe the world told you it wasn't cool. Maybe someone said that you could do better than that. Or maybe you just fell out of love with it at the moment because you were changing. All those reasons are valid. But honey, you know what else is valid? Changing your mind.

Often when we go back and pick up something we used to love, it's less about that thing—in my case, the flute—and more about how doing that thing made us feel. And I'm not going to tell you that those feelings are always going to be good. They might be amazing. I might play the flute and remember how much confidence it gave me. But those feelings might also remind you why you set that thing down. Why you stopped. That's okay, too. There are so many things that come with the territory of your new season, and sometimes on our freedom walk, we need those reminders of what not to return to.

And no, if you know without a shadow of a doubt that you put something down because it wasn't good for you, then don't you go picking it up again saying Tab told you to do it. If it wasn't serving you back then, and it caused you to not be well, honey, don't you go back to it. But if it's something you once loved and only lost because life got in the way, it might be worth a revisit.

I'm also not going to pretend that whatever your old-but-new thing is will be easy to take up again. Sure, maybe it will be like riding a bike and you'll pick back up where you left off—I know I hope it's like that for me and this flute. I'm certain that after some time it will come back to me, but I'm excited for the journey either way! Maybe the same will happen for you. Or maybe you'll have to learn it all over again. That's alright. The point is that you are rediscovering something about yourself. Something that you once loved. You may continue this new hobby or habit for the rest of your life or, as I said, you might stop next week. Either way, it's all good. Listen, Tab might take a few flute lessons and say, "No ma'am." But I know that nothing beats a failure like a try. I want to put forth the effort. I want to finish what I started. And I think you should, too!

We all love us some Lizzo, a classically trained flutist. But you better watch out! Tabbo may be coming soon!

TSA
(Tabitha Service Announcement)

*Starting over can be frustrating but know that
the strength and knowledge you gain from it can
also be your superpower!*

From Tab's "New Thing" Catalog

Go stargazing. Remember when you were little and you had no problem just lying in the grass on a warm summer night and looking up at the stars, pointing out the constellations and the moon? Well, honey, why not try that now? It's not just for kids. Or maybe it's the middle of the day and you grab a blanket, lay it out, and go cloud gazing! You can lay there solo or with a friend or partner and find all kinds of shapes in the clouds.

Build a fort. I don't know about you but me and my sister, oh my God, we were always building forts around the house. We'd build one in the basement with whatever pillows we could find and then put our sleeping bags and flashlights in there. Who says we can't recreate our childhood memories and grab a little bit of that joy for our adult lives?

Return to gym class. Remember that favorite sport you'd play in P.E. or gym class? Why not give it a shot again? Maybe it was dodgeball or volleyball. Whatever it was, tap back into that memory, gather some friends in a park, and try it again. You might find a new joyful hobby that you can also share with your community.

Do Something That Supports Someone Else

"I rejoice in the success of others,
knowing that there is plenty for us all."
—*Louise Hay*

I did a new thing.

I went to an eighteen-hole golf course for the very first time.

Notice I said "went to."

No, I did not *play* any golf at the golf course. But I did go to support my husband, Chance, in his very first celebrity golf tournament. More than anything, I went to be his cheerleader, supporter, and motivator. Look, Tab has no problem playing my position! I was the driver of the golf cart and an excellent cheerleader, and I loved every minute of it.

Most people who know me know that I have a passion for seeing people win. My daughter, Choyce, is always picking on me because I cry when I see people win. Oh my goodness, it just does my heart good. I love to see somebody go after their dream and win at it. It's such a good feeling!

That said, being able to truly be a cheerleader for someone requires a lot of self-discovery. We have to be honest with ourselves. When thinking about what it means to support someone else, ask yourself, "Do I normally just want people to cheer for me? Or do I have an issue with cheering for others?" If you struggle with supporting people, then it's time to do some work around that. If you're not cheering for other people, why not? I think sometimes we are fearful. We say, "If I cheer for somebody else, my dreams might not come true." Honey, let's go on ahead and call that thought what it is: a lie. Helping someone else is not going to stop you from getting whatever God has for you. If anything, it can encourage you to keep going. Your breakthrough might be connected to your ability to encourage and support somebody else.

To be clear: you do need to have a healthy balance when cheering for people or allowing people to cheer for you. *What do you mean by healthy balance, Tab?* Well, I mean before you allow yourself to cheer for someone else, make sure you are showing up for yourself first and foremost. You deserve to love on yourself and cheer yourself on as well. Then we can still be as supportive as we want people to be for us. Because honey, trust me. There will come a time when you will want people to show up for you, but if you don't show up for anybody else, if you don't cheer for other people, then they are going to remember that. We are in this world together, and at the end of the day, our support of those around us, especially those we love, is what we are here for.

I love cheering for Chance. I love that he has this new thing he loves called golf. He has his little golf bag, his hats, polo shirts, and spiked golf shoes. It all makes me so happy. Everybody needs something to look forward to, and this is his.

When you see somebody find their thing, something that brings them joy, cheer for them. Be excited for them. Because if God did it for them, He could do it for you. Your time is going to come. It just might be the other way around very soon. Somebody will be cheering and excited that you found your thing as well.

Now, back to this golf game: I just wish someone would have told me that an eighteen-hole golf game takes hours. *Hours?* Who knew? There's another level of patience one has to have to play at that level, but thankfully we could still have fun while being patient. In fact, it was amazing to me that the whole time we were there, the hours and hours and hours we rode around in those golf carts, we were also able to take breaks between holes. In the middle of the game, we stopped and got food and drinks. Sometimes the wind would be blowing too hard and we'd wait until the weather passed. When it calmed down and our hunger or thirst was satisfied, Chance and his group got right back into the game. Listen, honey, this was truly a new thing for me, because I'd never heard of anything like that before. I've been used to watching games where everyone is pressing toward the end. They are waiting for that buzzer to signal the game is over and doing everything they can to win until then. But God was using Chance's golf game to let me in on another secret to living free.

God was showing me that this game we . . . I mean, Chance . . . was playing is a lot like life. You have to be patient. You are not going to be able to rush your progress. Sometimes you might even have to wait out the bad weather. You will have to wait until the winds of your life calm down before you take your shot. But you can still have fun along the way. You can rest and take your time. Just like golf can be fun while you're playing it, life can be fun even as you're living it.

Another thing that came up for me was that I was watching Chance play this game when he'd been playing golf for only about six months. He was the newest player on the team, and for the last six months, he'd been practicing every week. He wasn't sure how he'd do playing alongside people who'd been playing for decades, but my Thundercat held his own! This helped me realize that consistency and practice go a long way. We may choose not to participate in things because we feel we haven't been doing the thing long enough, but honey, don't let fear of being new to something keep you from trying to hit the next level, okay? It doesn't matter how long you've been doing a thing as much as it matters how serious you take it. Everyone has a learning curve, but just because yours is longer doesn't mean you can't advance.

Honey, so what that you haven't been doing a thing for that long! Shoot, today could be your first day. The only one stopping you is you! I say, go about your business and try it. You may lose the game, but you'll still win the opportunity. I believe in you!

Listen, we are more than halfway through this book, so you must have figured out by now that Tab wants you to get comfortable with trying new things so that you can discover new ways to get to your personal freedom. So we are going to let go of those fears that are holding us back. We are going to release those anxieties and insecurities about how long we've been doing a thing or how we might compete. We're going to embrace the new things that may come our way because of the new things we do! God's got all of that covered. You just keep moving forward and creating a path that will lead you to new discoveries, alright?

TSA
(Tabitha Service Announcement)

Opportunities don't matter if you don't take advantage of them.

From Tab's "New Thing" Catalog

Send a card to a new entrepreneur. Know someone who has started a new business? Maybe your friend has begun a new venture and is feeling the weight that comes with doing her own new thing. Sending a note of encouragement could be the very pick-me-up they need to keep pursuing their dreams.

Show up to an event. Maybe your plans changed and while you thought you couldn't attend a friend's event, now you can. It would be such a wonderful surprise if you popped up there to support them.

Put on your chauffeur hat. Volunteer to drive someone to their engagement or event so they can focus on their moment and have a moment to take it all in. Oh, and while you're in the car, tell them how proud you are of them!

'Do Something That Pushes You Beyond Your Limits

"If you always put limits on everything you do, physical or anything else, it will spread into your work and into your life. There are no limits. There are only plateaus, and you must not stay there, you must go beyond them."
—*Bruce Lee*

I did a new thing.

I took Blacky, my dog, on a hike for the first time.

There was a point in my life when I used to hike daily. I'd fallen in love with hiking years ago when I began my healing journey.

I hadn't considered the mountains when I dreamed of moving to California. When you think about Hollywood, you think of lights, cameras, and stars, and mountains might never cross your mind. However, mountains surround the city, and they're always sitting there in the distance, waiting for you to climb. There's something so peaceful about moving through nature. The sounds of birds in the distance. Sharing space with the trees and other animals. There's also a deep quiet that I love. I can hear myself think. I can hear God. I am a witness to all of this, even in such a large city!

Although all those beautiful things I highlighted are true, hiking isn't easy. There were times early on when I've fallen on the trail and been very grateful that my brother was with me to help. Other times I'd just be too exhausted or weak to make it as far as I would like. But none of that mattered. None of that stopped me from going. Whenever I went hiking, it felt like I had the strength of God pushing me. I'd stare at the massive mountain and say, "Ooh honey, just like God created this massive mountain that cannot be moved, neither can I." And I'd use that strength to keep climbing on the mountain, and everywhere else in my life.

Over the last few years, though, I haven't hiked as much. First, the pandemic shut down a lot of the hiking trails for a good while. Then, my schedule got super busy, and ultimately, I wasn't able to hike as much as I used to. But today my brother said, "Let's go for a hike," and I was not only available, but I was down to go. I said, "You know what? Since we're going on an hour-long hike, I think I'm going to take Blacky, because he could use a long walk." My brother thought it was a great idea and brought his dog along, too.

Baby, when Blacky figured out that he was going farther than just around the neighborhood, he got so excited. He ain't but twenty-two pounds, but he pulled and yanked me up and down that mountain with a strength I didn't know he had. I'd never seen him so excited, so full of pure joy, with his tail wagging the entire time. Honey, I had to jog just to keep up with him! Most days, my brother Nic and I would just laugh, talk, and take our time. But Blacky was having none of that. He pulled me so hard that we got to the top in just over half the time. With my sweet dog's encouragement, I did more than I ever had before.

And that was it! Honey, when it came to hiking I'd been doing just enough to satisfy myself. I'd say, "Well, I know the trail is three miles, so I'll do three miles." But I never bothered to push myself. I never tried to cut down my time and hike the trail in forty-five minutes instead of an hour. And even while on the trail, I'd often stop frequently and take pictures or rest a little. But honey, today I did not stop. Blacky didn't let me. He was like, "Oh no, Mama, we're not stopping. I'm out here to see something new." All I could do was roll with him. He and I were both doing a new thing!

One of the main reasons many of us don't push ourselves beyond our self-imposed limits is because of fear. Yes, some of us are just comfortable, but most of the time it's because we are afraid. We say to ourselves, "I know that I'm good here. Ain't no need to do nothing else because I might fail if I keep going." That's it, right? We don't want to fail.

But honey, the problem with that is so much of what we call failure is based on what other people have said *to* us *about* us. We have based our ability to accomplish something, to fulfill our dreams, based on what the world has said about them. Well, baby, let me just say this: What others have said about you, all those things that keep you comfortable in staying still and not pushing yourself further, is a whole lie. The only real way to know whether something is going to work for you or if you have truly reached your limit is to actually try. To experience it for yourself.

And for those who aren't afraid and are just comfortable, it's time to own that, too—and release it. I know you've figured out that being comfortable doesn't require you to do anything hard. You can just keep doing things the same way you've always been doing them without much effort. But how's that working out for you, honey? You can't complain about your dreams not coming true or not reaching a goal if you aren't willing to stretch yourself and do something outside of your comfort zone. When we get too comfortable, we end up stagnant. When we don't move, we won't move, and then we can't see any farther than where we are. We lose any vision we might have had for our lives. And honey, that's a scary place for me. I don't want to live there. And I don't want that for you, either.

On this freedom walk, we all need to know that we deserve to have these new things. The new outlooks, new feelings, new rooms, and new joys are all yours if you want them. But the way we get to all that newness is by stepping outside of our comfort zones and stop believing the lies about our so-called limitations. But guess what? Do you know how much God loves us? Honey, God loves us enough to send a Blacky our way to push us. To remind us that we actually can do more. That we can go further. Who or what is your Blacky? Who is going to pull you along when you've become satisfied with the status quo?

Even as you are doing these new things daily, see if there are ways you can push yourself.

Now wait a minute, Tab is not telling you to be hard on yourself. It's not necessary to overdo it. Keep it small and simple. Do you normally walk thirty minutes on the treadmill? Great! Today see if you can add five minutes to your time. Too much? Okay, I understand. Like I said, don't overdo it. Try to add one more minute. It may not seem like much in the moment. It might not even seem worth it to do. But adding one more minute every other day just might have you walking an hour by the end of the year. So honey, set those small goals and allow them to push you like Blacky pushed me.

Today I realized that I had been playing with that mountain. That I'd always been able to do a little more but never made the attempt. And now, because I was open to learning even from my dog, God used him to teach me. To show me and you that when we allow ourselves to be truly excited about our new things, this uncharted territory God has placed us in, He might reveal that we've always been able to do more. That being and doing more was within our capability, but sometimes it takes us embracing our joy and being willing to listen to truly see that.

TSA
(Tabitha Service Announcement)

Speak life into your goals and dreams!
If you need a little push, remember the words
of Marvin Gaye and Tammi Terrell,
"Ain't no mountain high enough, to keep me
from getting to you." You got this!

From Tab's "New Thing" Catalog

Go roller or ice skating. Find your wheels (or blades), honey. If you are able, visit your local rink and have some fun skating. Not only is it fun, it's a great form of exercise.

Try a new exercise. I know you might be a Peloton girl. Or maybe your thing is CrossFit. But it can't hurt to try a new workout. You might actually find that the new exercises blend well with what you've been doing and incorporate it into your overall workout plans.

Try a new sport. Maybe you've never shot a basketball or kicked a soccer ball. Maybe you've been driving by those tennis courts and wondering what it might be like to get a racket and hit some balls. Don't be afraid of it. You're never too [insert whatever your fears are here] to try a fun new sport.

Meet My Play Cousin...
Nikki Did a New Thing

I don't think many people really realize just how many people were impacted by the COVID-19 pandemic. I'm not just talking about the terrible fact that over a million people died from the virus, but about those of us who lost our livelihoods as a result of the ongoing pandemic. My job was eliminated because, for whatever reason, the higher-ups weren't comfortable with us going to a virtual schedule. This didn't make any sense, because so many businesses at that time had gone to a work-from-home setup quite successfully, and many didn't even return to the office after getting the all clear.

When I lost my job, I felt so lost. It was like I was wandering aimlessly, trying to figure out what I would do next. I did have some severance I could live off for the remainder of the year, as well as some savings that I could tap into, but the last thing I wanted to do was deplete my savings without anything to replace income I lost. It was such a difficult time. At one point, especially after the severance ran out, I went into survival mode. I picked up odd jobs here and there to hold on. I had a child, and I wanted to make sure that we wouldn't have to leave our home or that I wouldn't have to sell my car. I mean, it really got tough.

But then I did a new thing. I started a business.

Honestly, I never thought I would be an entrepreneur. It just was never something I wanted to do. I came from a background where everyone worked a nine-to-five for thirty or forty years and then took retirement and a pension. That was the way I grew up. That was the way I thought you were supposed to do things. Yet, here I am, working for myself.

The interesting thing is that I have always had a passion for herbs and essential oils. I incorporated them into my life over a decade prior. My daughter, she's a teenager now, knows that Mommy always has an herbal remedy first before we go to the pharmaceutical route. To be clear: I don't have a problem with medicine or anything like that, but I always try to do something natural or holistic as a first line of defense. So herbs, oils, and holistic practices and remedies have been a part of my life for a very long time. But again, it never occurred to me that this passion I had, the thing I'd advocated for with family members who had been ill, or friends who were struggling with mental health challenges, could be something that would provide me a good living. Even during the pandemic, before we had vaccines or boosters, I utilized a lot of my knowledge of herbal remedies to help people who were dealing with respiratory issues and other symptoms of the virus. So it was like God had positioned me in this particular moment to be able to do this new thing, and help people and myself.

And I'm so glad He did. My business has been thriving for the last year, after only about a year of really hard work trying to get it off the ground. It wasn't easy. As a matter of fact, there were some days where I thought I should just try to go back into the workforce. But I think what was so amazing is that I had entered a perfect storm. There were all these stormy conditions—pandemic, my passion for herbal remedies, my ability to be at home in order to garden and grow the herbs myself—that created the right environment for this to be the natural next step in my life and career. I've learned that sometimes, the new thing we're supposed to do is actually the old thing that's always been present in our lives. And God wants to show us a new way to maximize that thing that's always been around. I'm so grateful that I listened.

Try a New Exercise or Workout—but Take Your Time

"You don't have to see the whole staircase,
just take the first step."
—*Rev. Dr. Martin Luther King Jr.*

I did a new thing.

I tried Pilates for the first time today.

Sure, after class I had to sit in the sauna for a good long time because of the way these muscles were mad at me, but I did it, y'all. I'm proud of myself, and honey, I absolutely loved it. I stretched myself in places I never knew could stretch, and it was worth it.

I'd heard so much about Pilates from friends and acquaintances who took classes, but I've never taken one myself before today. If I'm honest, it was because I was afraid of that machine. I don't know what I thought it was going to do to me, but I did know that I didn't want to find out. However, I finally agreed to take a class with some friends of mine, figuring that if I didn't like it, I never had to come back.

I almost didn't make it to class! I had shoots and meetings that ran over today and was running late. The class was only forty-five minutes, and I knew I wouldn't walk through the door until five minutes into the session. The easy thing for me to do would have been to text my friends saying, "Y'all know what? I'm running behind today. I ain't going to come to class because I don't want to be late." I mean, that's as good an excuse as any, right? But that's exactly what it would have been—an excuse. I took a minute to check myself and remember that even if I'm five minutes late, that still leaves me forty whole minutes to work out.

So I didn't think about it. I just drove to the studio and walked in the door, and to be honest I got nervous when I saw they had already started. My first thought was that I missed the instructions on how to get on the machine. The instructor motioned for me to come up front to the machine at the end of the row. She treated me like I was supposed to be there.

This was a moment for me. In the past, there were so many times when I was afraid to go to a gym and do any kind of workout out of the fear that I didn't know what I was doing and people would look at me like "Why are you here?" In that moment, I realized that it had all been in my head. The fact that she gave me a feeling of belonging was just what I needed for my trigger. So I jumped on the machine, excited to figure this thing out! The instructor took a moment to show me how to position myself and then she said, "Just follow along." I watched everybody and adjusted myself accordingly. The instructor came over a few times to properly position me when I made a wrong pose, which was so helpful and encouraging. It's like all my fears melted away and I was having fun learning something new; something I had been afraid of for so long! Honey, Tab has grown! I was late—I hate being late to anything—*and* I didn't know what I was doing, but I still showed up! I showed up for myself. I did something new, and my body was better for it.

Now, I ain't going to lie to you. Pilates hurts in some areas. But in a good way. Kind of like when you feel that slight pain from stretching but you also feel the relief and release in your muscles. Yes, like that. But at the end of the class I also felt like I climbed Mount Everest. Honey, I felt accomplished. I kept thinking, *Look at you, Tab. You did Pilates.*

And now, just like with many of the new things I've tried for this book, I think I might want to take up Pilates and go to classes a couple of times a week. No, I don't know if I'm going to become a Pilates girl. I'm not sure if my schedule will allow me to do a deep dive into it like I'd like to, but I'm excited about exploring it more and adding it to my workout routine. I want to see how it might change my body and even help me with my ongoing neck pain. It's totally possible that this one class, and my willingness to try something new, despite the obstacles that came my way, could change my life. It certainly helped me discover a new love.

Don't you love it when your new things lead to new loves? Honey, I do. But there's always a risk of overdoing something. If I run out and start doing Pilates seven days a week, that might be an overreaction to this new love I have for it. I might also end up injured. You see, discovering a new love is like trying a new piece of candy for the first time. It's sweet and yummy, but if we aren't careful, it can also hurt us. Some of us don't know when we've had enough. We eat too much candy and end up with a stomachache. But honey, I don't want that to stop you from trying something new.

I know that some of you aren't willing to try something new, not because you are scared something bad will happen, but because you're actually scared that you might like that thang too much. Everyone wants to know that we can pull ourselves away from something. I get that. And yes, there is some self-discipline we all need to learn as we are trying our new things and taking these leaps of faith. But don't give up on the possibility of discovering something you love simply because you might really like it. Just do what you need to do, honey, to safeguard yourself as you are enjoying it.

I've actually noticed this same thing with people who are scared to date. I'm sure that part of them is afraid of getting their heart broken, but I think what many are really afraid of is falling in love and maybe *too* quickly. They are afraid of the responsibilities that come with a good love. They don't want to be held accountable by someone else for their actions when it comes to this new thing. They don't want someone telling them they are doing too much or too little, and they've let other people tell them what that "much" and "little" is. But the problem with that is that they're giving control of their happiness to someone else.

So what if loving somebody new means we have to be held

accountable? We actually might need that. Or maybe we can just hold ourselves accountable to our own standards. Maybe we say, "You know what? I fell in love with this person and right now I'm liking them a whole lot." We hold on to our truth even if there are others who think we are doing too much or being extra in our relationships. Even if there are those who think we aren't doing enough, or not giving enough of ourselves. There will always be people with an opinion about how we live our lives. Some of those opinions are important to at least listen to. Many of them are not. The beautiful thing about doing a new thing and, as a result, discovering a new love is that *we* get to decide what we do about that. We get to say, "Yes, I'm doing too much with this new love in my life, but that's my business." We also get to say, "You know what? I did love that thing but I'm also going to take it bit by bit and see what happens. I'm not ready to jump in all at once but when I am, I will."

There's a sweeter side to trying and loving that candy. When you aren't overdoing it, it does your body and mind good. It gives you a little bit of energy and a small hit of joy. So when we have a little balance, a new piece of candy that we love will never disappoint us. Like that strawberry candy with a little bit of filling in it that our aunties and grandmas used to give us at church—your new thing, that new love, may or may not last forever, but if you take your time and savor it slowly, it's always worth it.

Which brings me to one more thing: Not only did I have to believe that I could do this new thing and then be willing to show up for myself, but the one thing Pilates taught me today was to slow down. You can't rush when you are stretching your body on those machines. I mean, you can try it if you want to, but that's not going to end well, alright? And y'all know Tab was in there just moving fast. At least until the instructor said something that hit me like a ton of bricks. She said, "You need to slow down. The slower your movement, the quicker you tone." *Okay, God! I hear you!*

The truth is, some of us are moving too fast and wondering why we aren't getting the results we desire. That's probably because the results we desire *can't* happen the way we are moving. If we slow down, pace ourselves, and move just a little bit slower, then we will know that we are doing things the right way and our results will actually be quicker. Y'all know what happens when you're moving too fast? You miss some stuff. You're likely to find yourself messing up along the way. That's inevitably what happens when we rush. But as the instructor said, the slower you move, the quicker you tone. Your life will respond more favorably when you are taking your time and paying attention. So I encourage you to take your time in discovering your new thing—and just wait to see the beautiful results!

TSA
(Tabitha Service Announcement)

*Slow and steady wins the race, but only if you
get on your mark, get set, and go!*

From Tab's "New Thing" Catalog

Watch the sun rise or set. I didn't realize there were so many people who had never seen the sun come up or set until that question was asked at a recent conference I attended. Honey, if you ever needed to just slow down, pace yourself, and focus on your breath, watching the sun rise or set will definitely help you with that.

Take a very long walk in a new place. Whether it is the next neighborhood over, a different part than you're used to, or an entirely new city, take the time to find a new place to be outside and walk.

Bake a dessert. Honey, I've said many times that baking ain't my ministry. But I do know that if you want to do something that will force you to take your time and build patience, baking is it. And there's a tasty payoff at the end, too!

Dance in the Rain (Yes, You Too, Black Girl)

I did a new thing.

Honey, me and Donna went running in the rain.

For the last few weeks, California has had enormous and unusual amounts of rain. Honey, I know Tony! Toni! Toné! said "It never rains in Southern California," but baby, they were wrong! For two weeks we've had nothing but rain, floods, mudslides, and even a blizzard or two. Now normally, I try to stay out of the rain. I don't like getting muddy or dirty, and I'm from the South, where we are conditioned to believe the old wives' tale that says if you get your head wet, you'll get sick. Plus, Donna don't be feeling the rain, and I can't say that I blame her. But today, for whatever reason, God said, "Tab, go stand in the rain."

Um, okay. If you've followed me for any length of time, then you know that I try to move when God says move. Obedience to the Spirit has been the key to living free for me. So I got right on up when I heard God say in my heart, "Listen, I send the rain to cleanse. I want you to step outside and allow yourself to feel that just for a little bit. Walk around in it." Now yes, I may or may not have protested a little bit because, as I said, Lord knows that Donna and I don't like to walk around in no rain. But then God hit me with "Tab, I want you to feel something that no one else can create and really just have a moment with it." And, honey, I did just that.

I stopped all the chatter in my mind. I quieted all the negative voices worried about sickness and hair and wet clothes. I stepped outside into my yard and just allowed myself to take it all in. Have you ever really sat and listened to the sound of rain? Honey, it's so beautiful. I can hear the music in it. As a matter of fact, I heard laughter in all the pitter-patter of the rain against the ground and trees and plants. I stood there as the rain drenched me from head to toe and allowed the beauty of this creation of God to overtake me. And then it happened. I felt a release like never before.

You know how you might be standing in the shower and somehow the water hitting you in your face just takes your mind off whatever might be going on outside those tiled walls? You can't even think about the chaos of the world because the water is so soothing? Well, let's just say it was like that multiplied by a thousand. I'm pretty sure it was because I wasn't in control. I couldn't just turn the knob and shut off the water whenever I wanted to. Standing outside, there was no doubt that God was in control of the rain—and my life. He could surely stop it at any time, but I didn't have any say on when that would be. So my heart just surrendered to His will. "Listen, Tab," God continued speaking to my heart.

"I want you to look at your life the same way you're looking at this rain. These blessings I'm pouring down on you? I'm the one who controls them. Don't you try to control a single thing. Just let the rain fall and trust that it's Me doing it." What a powerful word, and one that confirmed what I'd been hearing for a while.

Many years ago, I was speaking at a high school graduation and as I was standing at the podium telling my story, I realized that, in that moment, I was pretending to be somebody else. I was trying to create this other persona in order to be successful, to win in the ways I thought I should. It was crystal clear that God was saying, "I can't give you what I want to give you because you ain't you." Honey, I must admit I was shocked but not surprised. Because He was right. God can't bless who we pretend to be because He doesn't know that person. He can't give us what He needs to give us until we choose to be who He created us to be. So we have to be very careful when we try to create an image that we think the world wants or we try to control every aspect of our lives, thinking that's the way we can get what we desire. Baby, no, that's not how it works at all.

One of the greatest compliments I receive is from all the play cousins I meet at various events across the country, who later post on social media, "Tabitha is exactly the same person you see online." Because that means I've been obedient to God and who He created me to be. I'm being exactly myself and in turn, God can continue to bless me.

When we try to take the ultimate control of our lives and leave no room for God to work, what we are really saying is that we don't trust God. You might as well tell Him that He didn't do a good job. That the you He created isn't good enough. But what we don't realize is being someone else is exhausting and a ridiculous way to live. When we truly decide to let God be in control and do what He has called us to do, then that trust will always lead to Him blessing us with what we deserve—which, honey, is more than we could ever imagine. Ask Tab how she knows!

So how do you put yourself in a posture to receive God's rain? Well, baby, you've got to be honest about where you are. Look at your life and see if you are where you believe you are supposed to be. And if you're not, then the next step will probably require some changes on your part. You might have to move. You might have to stop doing some of the things you used to do. You might have to try something new (good thing you got this book).

I'm a whole witness, y'all. As soon as I decided that the Tab I was trying to be wasn't working, that I'd been hustling hard for something and still had nothing to show for it because I wasn't being myself, God said, "Let me show you something. If you just trust me, trust the you that I made you to be . . . when you do that, everything will change." And it did. My life today is drastically different from the one I had even three years ago. I'm blessed beyond measure.

God knows us better than we know ourselves. And I understand that trusting that is not always easy. Trying to stop being a control freak is hard. But I believe that God will honor our trying. There will be days when you'll have to take more time to breathe. You'll have to say, "This typically isn't what I'd normally do, but that's okay." It will work out for you. Remember, I never wanted to do anything with food. I'm a trained actress. I moved to California to pursue acting. When I arrived, I had vision boards and journals that chronicled my journey to becoming an actress. Not a single entry or image had anything to do with food. But God clearly told me to start doing videos. "Tell people what you're eating. Show them what you're cooking," He said. And of course, I wasn't happy. I didn't want to do that. I wanted to act. And God said, "Who are you trusting, Tabitha? Are you trusting you or are you being obedient to what I have told you?" Honey, I got right to making videos. And those videos changed my life. They have led me to acting plus doing way more than I could have imagined. Read that again. Obedience and trying something new changed everything.

Honey, it took everything in me today to not break out into a dance in that rain. Next time I probably will. I was as full in my spirit as my clothes and hair were wet. And I would have missed it all if I didn't choose to do something new, check the voices of resistance, and go where I was told to go. Plus, now I get to share that word with you. No, you don't get to control the rain. Yes, sometimes the rain comes in the form of blessings and sometimes it comes in the form of utter disaster. But I want you to stand there in it and trust the God who allowed it to pour. Because even in the worst of storms, there is beauty when it ends. There's growth—just ask the flowers and the grass. They know.

So let's not run away from the rain or always try to take cover. Sometimes we need to embrace it. Allow it to cleanse us from the things we may not even see. Allow it to hydrate the areas of our lives that have been dry for way too long. Honey, allow it to bring some things back to life. The rain taught me today that it can feel just as good as the sun if we change our mind about it. Go walk, run, laugh, or dance in the rain just one good time. Then wait for your overflow.

TSA
(Tabitha Service Announcement)

You deserve love, in the rain and the sunshine!

From Tab's "New Thing" Catalog

Ask for a raise. I know, you're nervous. You have all these thoughts running through your head about what you will say or what they will say in response. Baby, if you don't go on ahead and walk into that office and ask for what you deserve. Or ask for that meeting with that very important person who might be able to help you reach your goals. Nothing beats a failure like a try.

Present your idea. Tell somebody you trust, someone who believes in you, about that idea you have. Stop holding it in and being afraid of what might happen. Speak it now so it can be in the atmosphere. That's only one stop away from it coming to be.

Execute one step in your dream plan. Do your research on business formation; go ahead and get that LLC. Apply for your passport. Honey, while you're at it, run your credit and see if you can get approved for that mortgage. So many people are too afraid to even see where they are in order to know what to do next. Not you. Not anymore.

Make Time for Old Friends

"We'll be friends forever, won't we, Pooh?'
asked Piglet. 'Even longer,' Pooh answered."
—*A.A. Milne*, Winnie the Pooh

I did a new thing.

I made time for old friends.

Honey, for the last few years, I have been working, working, working. And when I'm not working, I spend much of my time with my family. But there are times when I miss the slower days. The days when I'd go for a hike with friends. The days when I'd dream about the opportunities I have now and share those dreams with my hiking buddies. I haven't had time for that in a long while, and so much of my life is scheduled, so when some of my old hiking friends decided to get together, I jumped at the chance to do something I hadn't done in a long time.

It started when I ran into my old friend Karen, at the nail shop. We hadn't seen each other in forever, and it was so good to hug her. I'd met her about six years prior as I was coming out of my illness. She was the first person who taught me how to hike.

Even as I think about how I arrived to where I am today, I can't help but remember how she was a part of my journey. She knew I'd been sick but didn't really know how sick. And yet, God allowed her to be in my life, to be that person who pushed me to be outside more. The days we hiked, I always felt so good afterward, and it created an urgency in me to continue healing.

"Oh, Tab. Me and Carlin miss you so much," she said.

Carlin is another friend of mine who I met through Karen. We always used to go to the gym together. For three or four days a week, Karen, Carlin, and I would hike together on the mornings I felt up to it, while the kids were at school. On the days I didn't feel so great, we would all take our time climbing the mountain, because Carlin also was a cancer survivor who had problems with her knees. So just imagine the three of us—women, mothers— hiking and talking. We shared so much on those trails. We talked about our day-to-day issues and our love for our children and families. They are both seven to ten years older than me, which isn't surprising. My whole life, I've always been drawn to older people. But I so appreciated their wisdom in that season of my life and was grateful for all they poured into me.

So when I saw Karen at the salon, she said, "We've got to get together."

"You know what? We've got to do lunch or breakfast or something before my schedule gets super crazy."

And we left it at that.

I thank God for Karen, because she was on it. Honey, she sent a text out to our little group on a Thursday and said, "How about coffee?" Unfortunately, I had to say no because I was traveling. But I continued looking at my calendar because I was determined to make this happen. Too many times I get in work or family mode and forget that I need my friends, too. Finally, I said "I'm available on Saturday." Karen texted back "How about breakfast?" And I was there! Yes, it was Saturday and even if I wasn't working, I could have easily said, "No, I need to rest on that day." But I didn't. I stepped out of my new comfort zone and said, "You know what? I need some of that old energy. It was once very good for me."

And it was.

We met that morning at this super cute, Black-owned café called *The Kitchen* in Granada Hills, which was a central location for all of us. We were sitting at the window and it was actually raining, but the rain was just so peaceful. It made for such a good moment with us. It felt like things were exactly how they were supposed to be. Baby, we had a good ol' time. My soul woke up and was fed. We laughed, we cried, we truly caught up on life, and it was beautiful!

We've been able to keep in touch since that meet-up, which is great. I've begun to think about how many of us need reminders of the times when things were much slower or easier. Honey, we should never put off spending time with the people and things that helped shape our journeys, the ones who helped us along our way without even knowing their true impact. They matter in our story, and sometimes you have to tell them or remind them how big a role they played in your life. There's something so beautiful about pure friendships, sisterhoods and brotherhoods. The pure love we get from people who know us and want nothing from us. I sat in that restaurant with two beautiful women as we bonded and loved on each other. There were tears and laughter, and most of all, a sense that we all needed each other in that moment. We didn't have to wonder if someone was going to tear another person down because all of us were focused on building each other up.

It's too easy to forget about friends who may not have known you since childhood, but who might have popped up later in your life. Yes, y'all know Tab believes that friendships have seasons, but what I also know is true is that authentic, reciprocal friendship will have room for restoration. And when you do reconnect, it will likely feel like no time was ever lost. The feelings are still the same.

I know my life changed drastically, and that some of my friends haven't had such a dramatic shift. It was so funny to hear them say things like, "We can't believe that we know you. We're always like, 'That's our Tab!'" But at the end of the day, no matter where we are in our lives, we all have our personal struggles. And it's often your sisters and friends who will take the time to hear you. To see you. We can talk to each other and love on each other in a very special way. Meeting with the ladies reminded me of how special those moments can be, especially when the people have true, genuine love for you and there's no judgment, hate, or jealousy. That's really hard to find.

Make sure that when you know you have true friends who love and celebrate you, you take time to have a moment with them. When you're available, make it happen. Do something new with them. Today was the first time I'd ever been to that restaurant. Karen had suggested it. I've now been back two times. Sometimes your something new will come from reaching out to your friends, and honey, that's more than okay, too.

So I encourage you today to tap in with your old friends (if they were healthy friends, of course). Maybe phone an old friend or reach out and ask an old colleague to lunch. Try to connect with someone you haven't been able to connect with because everyone is so busy. It really does bring back some beautiful feelings, and it can also inspire you to be excited for something new again.

TSA
(Tabitha Service Announcement)

True friendship never dies.

From Tab's "New Thing" Catalog

Schedule that dinner with your childhood friend. I can't stress enough the importance of reconnecting with those healthy friendships from your past. Not every relationship stops because of something terrible happening. Sometimes friendships just fade because of time and distance. But you might be able to change that. Start today.

Make time for some one-on-one time—with yourself. Read that book on your TBR list. Watch that show you've been wanting to dig into. I know you're always taking care of others, but today, take care of you. You're worth it!

Take yourself shopping. Again, I know you shop for the kids or the house or your parents. But what if you take *you* on a shopping spree? And if money is tight, honey, the dollar store can still be a real good time. Go buy some dollar bubbles and have some play time! It will do the body good.

Meet My Play Cousin ...
Paula Did a New Thing

This year, I celebrate my twenty-fifth high school class reunion. When my former classmates sent the information about all the planned festivities, I just stared at the email. I had no intention of going. I wanted to, but I was terribly busy. My job took me overseas and all over the country visiting different college campuses and doing recruitment for our graduate programs. I didn't think there was any way I could make time for a class reunion and still do my job well, take care of my family, and wear all the other hats I wore.

But admittedly, something inside me was pulling at me. I longed to reconnect with some of my friends from back in high school. There were a couple of girls who were on the drill team with me that I was really tight with, but who I hadn't seen in many, many years. I was curious not just about their lives but how they were doing, and was praying and hoping that all was well, especially in light of the state of the world nowadays. Still, I just couldn't see how to make time for this event considering my busy schedule.

Then, a few days after that initial itinerary email, I got another one from the reunion committee that rocked me to my core. It was an announcement that the vice president of our class, a kind, sweet girl who everyone loved—just a real good person—had passed away. I couldn't believe it. We were too young for these kinds of conversations. Who is passing away suddenly at forty? But it was an eye-opener, to say the least. It shook me to the point where I said, "You know what? I'm not going to waste any more time. I'm not going to work myself into the ground and not see any of the fruit of that work because I don't allow myself any time to rest or to laugh or to dance." I RSVP'd to attend my reunion and sent in my fee.

It wasn't what I intended to do, but there's something about loss and grief, even from people who you may not be super close to, that changes you on the inside. It makes you realize that life is too short. We work so much. We invest a lot in trying to ensure that our kids have enough money to go to college or that we have the right house in the right neighborhood. But how are we investing in our own souls and well-being? Part of that means being in a community with people. And yeah, I have friends at home. I have a strong community that I am proud to be a part of, neighbors I regularly say hi to on my way to work. But there are people that I grew up with who know me from way back, and who can speak to a part of me that the people in my life now just can't. And that's okay. My mindset had completely shifted. I was now looking forward to attending this reunion.

On the very first night that I arrived in my hometown of Jacksonville, Florida, there was a meet and greet. From across the room, I saw Nicole, one of those girls who was on the drill team with me. But she's not a girl now. She's a gorgeous woman. And she looked at me from across the room and screamed like Beyoncé had walked in behind me. "Oh my God, I can't believe it's you!" She ran over to me and hugged me so tight. Something about her touch just shot me right back to being sixteen years old. The memory of us going on our trip to a competition in Orlando and getting on the bus. All the secrets we told each other about the boys we liked and the teachers we didn't. It just all rushed back to me and filled me with so much joy.

Me and Nicole talked for most of that meet and greet. Catching up with her was the most amazing time. The same for my chat with Tommy, the crush I had as a sophomore, whose wife is gorgeous. And even some of the conversations with my so-called enemies were enlightening. I marveled at how people change and how, as much as I wanted people who knew me back then to speak to that childlike part of me, there were also people there who clearly had changed for the better. That was so good to see. I think it could have been easy to try to judge some of those people based on who they once were, but I couldn't bring myself to do. We were all different. The same, but also different.

Going to my class reunion was my new thing, and it couldn't have come at a better time. It was a revelation to set aside my schedule and all the things I thought I had to do in order to take a minute to just love on myself and the people who were part of my past.

Exchange Your Craving for Something Healthy

"A journey of a thousand miles begins
with a single step."
—Lao Tzu

I did—am doing—a new thing.

I'm fasting from potatoes and bread, for myself and in memory
of my mom. She used to fast from potatoes every year for Lent
because she loved them so much. So, Moma, this one is for you!
I'm fasting from bread as well because I realized I'd been indulging
a little too much. So I tried a new food that is helping with that.

It's so interesting to me how, when you let a certain food go, your cravings for that food get stronger before they go away. It's like your taste buds just decide to turn things all the way up in a last-ditch effort to stop you from giving up this thing you know you love but you also know might not be good for you. At least that's what's been happening to me since I started the fast. As much as I love potatoes and bread, I also know that too many starchy carbohydrates aren't great for me and my system, especially since I'm always on the go and don't really have time for the carb crash that comes with them.

But tonight I tried Japanese squash, also called kabocha, and—ooh God I thank you. Now, honey, I've tried many different types of squashes, but the funny thing about this one is that it looks very much like a pumpkin when it comes to shape, but tastes nothing like it. The vegetable itself is green with spots on it, but when you bite into it, I promise, you'll think you're eating a whole potato. The one I had was baked and stuffed with mushrooms and, baby, you couldn't tell me I wasn't eating a sweet potato/Idaho combo. In fact, I was so stunned by how similar to potatoes the squash tasted that I thought I was doing something wrong. Like I'd messed up my fast or something.

You see, I have been missing everything about potatoes. I don't care if it's sweet potato, mashed potato, French fries, potato chips, or, honey, hot potato, I could tear into any of them right now if it wasn't for this fast. So to come across this kabocha that tastes like the very thing I've been craving—well, I feel like I won a new prize! And isn't that it? When you try something new, sometimes you find out that the very thing you thought you couldn't do without has a replacement that is not only just as good to you, it's also good for you. Because y'all know Tab looked up the health benefits of the Japanese squash, right? Yes, I did.

Kabocha improves blood sugar levels and is lower in calories and carbs than a sweet potato. Studies have shown that it helps prevent cancer growth, decreases blood pressure, and protects heart, eye, and skin health. Who knew? There are so many benefits to this vegetable that I would have likely never tried had I not been challenging myself to fast. And now I have something that I will keep as part of my mental list of healthy options. When I have a taste for potatoes or sweet potatoes but know that I'm trying to be a little bit healthier, I now know I have other options. I look forward to making more recipes with kabocha. Maybe I'll stuff it like a regular potato with vegan butter and sour cream.

Sometimes you have to try a new thing to replace an old thing. It can help distract you from any old habits that might be hard to break, at least until you have the strength to know that you can be good without the old thing. Trying something new out of curiosity can actually help you to develop new, healthier habits. Like, in my case, overeating potatoes. But the only way to discover if something new can be better for us is if we have an open mind and are willing to release the old thing. Because, honey, ain't that it? Eating this kabocha wouldn't matter as much if I wasn't willing to let go of the potatoes for a season. We're so conditioned to hold on to stuff, especially when it comes to our food. Most people don't see food as an addiction, but for some people it can be a real thing. So the reset is often necessary.

The reset can help us heal. It can give us peace of mind because sometimes it ain't just about food. It's about what's in our minds.

It's about what we've been telling ourselves. Have you ever thought you needed something or someone and realized after it or they were gone that you really didn't? I know I've said, "Oooh, I need some potatoes. I need some comfort food," but now I know a better way to get that "comfort" without overindulging. Yes, Tab loves a potato. It feels and tastes good. But there is something better for me. So I shift my mindset and say to myself, "No, girl, you've got to release that."

I've said this before but I'm going to say it again—there's something amazing about opening up your palate to something new. It's not only the immediate benefits of a new food, it's also what we unknowingly tell our minds and bodies in the process. In a way that is simple and easy to access—our taste—we tell our bodies that we are open to new things in all areas of our lives. In this case, I was able to tell my body that I can fulfill my cravings without hurting myself or going against a promise I made to myself and God—in this case, the fast. Honey, that's a whole word right there. You can still keep your promise while doing something new that fulfills whatever void you think you have.

TSA
(Tabitha Service Announcement)

*Sometimes you might find something new
that takes the edge off, while missing
the thing you released.*

From Tab's "New Thing" Catalog

Replace a milkshake with a smoothie. You love your sweets, I know. But you can still have it, only just a little bit healthier. Mangoes, strawberries, and kiwi just might give you the same kick you like.

Exchange fried for baked or grilled. I know that fried mushrooms be calling you. It's okay to send them to voicemail sometimes. Grilled mushrooms can get all your face time today.

Exchange your juices or teas or lemonade . . . for water. Yes, I know, I know. But hear me out. Water will not only hydrate you, but it will help you feel better mentally. You won't get that sugar drop that comes a couple of hours after juice or lemonade and often leads to fatigue or irritation. Let's choose water as our drink of the day.

Try a New Scent

"Only those who will risk going too far can
possibly find out how far one can go."
—*T.S. Eliot*

I did a new thing.

I bought a new perfume.

When I was little, I remember seeing all the glass bottles on my mama's closet dresser. They were all different shapes and sizes with all kinds of labels on them. Honey, my mother loved her some perfume. But the funny thing is, I didn't really get into perfume when I was younger. But now? Listen, I love perfume now. There's something about having a signature scent or two that makes me feel like a grown woman. And most of the time, I don't deviate from my favorite ones. I mostly like to use scents to help me create memories. Like when I'm shooting *Tab Time*, my children's show, I wear a perfume called Soul Cafe and everyone knows it's my scent.

I like to think about how, in the future, I can smell a scent and it will bring me back to a specific moment in time.

But today, while still in Miami, I decided to do a new thing and try a new scent. In the hotel where we are staying, there's a space that has a bunch of different perfumes that you can try on and purchase. My first thought was to buy one of my favorite scents, an old standby, but then I came across one that absolutely blew my mind: Byredo's Mojave Ghost.

With one whiff, I was transported back in time. The scent reminded me so much of my mama. I felt her presence so strong when I sprayed the perfume that I suddenly got quiet. I was near tears. I know the salesperson was wondering what was going on. This happy, smiling, talkative woman walks into her store and suddenly goes quiet, staring off into the distance, spraying a perfume? That was probably weird. After a minute, I looked at her and said, "My mom passed away, and this smells so much like her." That's when her face changed. She understood.

Now, I'm sure Moma never wore this particular perfume, but for whatever reason, it made me think of her. It smelled like her. I closed my eyes and let the scent take me over. Honey, I promise it felt like a warm hug from Heaven. Then I said to the clerk, "Girl, I'll take it. Matter of fact, give me two bottles because I know this is going to be a favorite." Instant sale.

I also noticed that the brand offered a matching hair mist, so I asked for that also. Baby, I wanted it all. But unfortunately they didn't have it there.

"Oh, they sell it in Nordstrom's," she said.

So the hunt began.

I went to Nordstrom's and they said, "Oh, we don't have it. They have it at Neiman's."

Then I went to Neiman-Marcus.

After some investigation from the salespeople there, I finally found the hair mist, and you would have thought they'd told me I'd won an Oscar. I was overjoyed. I have every intention of wearing this scent often, and especially when I'm missing my mama. And isn't it just crazy that the name of the perfume is Mojave Ghost? The idea that I get to feel her spirit all around me makes me feel so full.

In a way, the scent of that perfume opened up a portal for me. I know, I know. Some people get nervous when they hear me use that word. "Oh wait, you messing with witchcraft, Tab?" But what they don't understand is that any time we talk about life or death— whether that's a physical living and dying or the life and death of parts of ourselves—we are talking about moving from one dimension to the next. One state of being to the next. And that space where we cross over can be seen as a portal. I truly believe that sometimes we can open up a side of us that we have never, ever felt before by stepping outside of our comfort zone. In the same way we work out and start to use new muscles, we can use a new part of our brain and see growth.

Honey, when I was on that Pilates machine, I know I used muscles and ligaments I've rarely used that way before. By doing that, I opened a new part of me. Gave my body a new opportunity for healing and strength. And yes, I was sore. It wasn't comfortable to do that new thing, but that slight discomfort was a sign that what I was doing was working.

Too many of us don't realize that when we do something new, we are stretching our minds to a place it's never been. As a result, our bodies, our mentality—everything changes. Expanding the space in your brain with memory or movement does open a portal. A space where you can cross over from one state of living to the next. From bondage to freedom. When I decided to try Mojave Ghost, it unlocked a part of my mind where my memories were held. Memories of my mama. While she's no longer here, I experienced the gift of her presence in that moment.

This "new thing" has triggered so many wonderful memories for me. And sometimes that's the point. We don't always have to look for the deep word or meaning in these efforts to try something new. Sometimes doing something you'd ordinarily not do simply puts you in a position to receive something sweet. Like a nod from Heaven. Like the memory of wonderful days gone by. These are all gifts from the other side.

The fact that trying a new perfume opened up so much for me makes sense when you think about how our bodies work. Certain smells can trigger intense emotions and, I would say, connect us to the parts of us that want to remember. Even sounds and certain kinds of music can send us messages from the other side.

It makes me smile to think about how present our loved ones who've passed on are in our lives when we allow them to be. If we keep our eyes, minds, hearts, and apparently our noses open to experiencing them in a different way, we will ultimately allow them to bring memories to us. I know that's what my mama did today. That nudge to walk into the store was definitely from her. I'm not sure I had any intention of buying anything today, but I ended up finding a new favorite scent that I will now cherish for a very long time. Thank you, Moma.

TSA
(Tabitha Service Announcement)

It's easy for people to tell you that your experiences with spirit don't make sense and it's even easier for them to call you crazy. Don't believe them! You are not crazy, and spirit is real.

From Tab's "New Thing" Catalog

Play the blindfold game. Explore your senses by getting some friends together, blindfolding everyone one at a time, and seeing who can recognize various scents. Start with perfumes and essential oils. Do you know what lavender smells like? Frankincense? Then you can move on to food. Put several different kinds of food up to a person's nose and let them guess what it is. You can also do this with drinks. If you really want to have some fun, try to recognize various sounds and voices. Was that a door shutting or a cabinet slamming? Is that my sister or my cousin? This is a super fun way to open yourself up to the new feelings, energy, and superpowers that come from tapping into your senses.

Prepare Well for Your New Thing

> "The challenge is not to be perfect—it is to be whole."
> —*Jane Fonda*

I did a new thing.

I went snowmobiling today.

And I got a cold.

Honey, I was looking forward to snowmobiling in the Utah mountains. I was there for work but made some time for a little fun and playtime with my husband. Y'all didn't know Tab was a bit of a daredevil, huh? Well, I am. And I planned to add snowmobiling to my list of adventures I've conquered.

Honey, I had a ball while I was out there, but when I came back to the room and my whole throat was on fire, I knew that my adventure had gone left in a big way. Apparently having on a full ski suit wasn't enough. I didn't wear the proper mask to cover my neck, and all the wind and snow in my face and nose messed me up something terrible. If I'd had the proper protection, I probably would have been just fine.

So of course, as God does, I received a few good messages in the midst of it all. See, it was our first time snowmobiling and we didn't know what to expect. Before we even got to the site, it started to snow really hard. I was already having difficulty breathing because the elevation is so high in those mountains. So when our driver started questioning us about going out in that weather, we started to get nervous. She said, "We are experiencing record-breaking lows today and people don't normally snowmobile in these conditions."

"Uh-oh, is this going to be a good idea or not?"

But we pressed on.

We felt a little bit better when we arrived because there were a bunch of people waiting. Plus the instructor was giving us a private session.

"Don't worry," she said. "It's going to be great. This is soft snow, so it's all right."

And so we geared up. I really thought a helmet, goggles, and my cowl-neck scarf were all I needed, but I soon realized there is a reason we see people who do mountain sports wearing a full ski mask that covers their neck. No, I just kept thinking I didn't need all that.

I did.

So we headed out and the instructor began giving us the lay of the land. She told us that she would give us hand signals because the motors were too loud as we were moving.

"If you see me throw up a fist, that means stop exactly where you are because there's a mother moose and her baby. Mama Moose is not happy about our snowmobiles and can go into protection mode. As she should. As soon as you see the fist, get down in front of your windshield because if she charges, she's going for the front of the vehicle."

Lord Jesus, we are in her house. We are on her land. Please don't let us run into her.

Honey, Tab was praying, alright? And thankfully, we didn't see her while we were on the snowmobile. But while we were in the car getting ready to leave the facility, we saw a moose moving off in the distance. It was the baby! And while we didn't see the mama, I'm pretty sure she was nearby. I kept thinking, *If the baby is this big, the mama must be huge.*

"Let's get out of here," I said. I wasn't messing with mama moose for one second.

Seeing baby moose gave me even more respect for nature. See, the truth is, mama moose was only doing what she's supposed to do: protect her child in her home. It got me thinking so much about how we really should do our best to honor nature, including the animals that live in it. Enjoy the beauty of the natural world, yes, but let's also leave it the way we found it. Don't mess it up.

Even though the thought of a mama moose charging us was very scary, snowmobiling in the mountains was the most beautiful experience for me. Honey, Mother Nature was in her element.

The scenery was breathtaking. Yes, it was a wild ride being so high up, but to witness God's creation up close was such a blessing. To see snow more than fifteen feet high and mountain neighborhoods that were not allowed to have cars, just snowmobiles, was mind blowing! We saw houses literally buried under the snow. Only the tip of street signs peeking out of the drifts. It felt like we were in a whole new world! As we were coming out of the neighborhood tour, we saw a woman digging her snowmobile out of a carport and the instructor told us that that was absolutely normal. I couldn't believe it! But something about that seemed so peaceful. She wasn't rushing, she was taking her time, and as we rode by, she offered a wave and a smile! Again, it was all so beautiful!

I just wished I was better prepared. Although I was taking in all this newness and amazing scenery, my neck and throat were so cold. My face was freezing, and I was starting to feel a little dizzy.

That was the lesson for me today. I had this amazing moment, but I was not all the way prepared for it. If I'd just taken a moment to prepare myself properly, to put on the proper ski mask, then I wouldn't have this terrible cold. The experience would have been even more enjoyable than it was.

Yes, I know what you're thinking: "Tab, the cold doesn't make you sick, germs do." Well, honey, all I know is that snow made my neck and throat become extremely sore, and it was hard to swallow afterward. So I'm going with not being prepared for the snowmobiling made me sick, alright?

The bottom line is this: there might be something amazing on the other side of our adventures, but if we aren't properly prepared, we might also find ourselves hurt. We may also lose that gift altogether.

Sometimes doing something new without any preparation, without thinking about it first, means that your experience will be short-lived. I remember when I was so excited to get a new car. I wanted a Mercedes so bad. Then I finally got the Mercedes but realized I wasn't prepared for the cost of its maintenance. The gas price was higher. The tires cost more. And when the car broke down, the repair cost was out of this world. Honey, I did a new thing and got my favorite car, but because I wasn't financially prepared to take care of it, it caused more problems, more hurt and harm, than it was worth. That car not only created financial strain but it also caused many arguments in my home.

So that's it, y'all. We have to be prepared in every way—mentally, physically, financially—for our something new. In all the new things we've done over the course of almost thirty days, I would never suggest you do something that will ultimately hurt you. Yes, discomfort is fine. We need some of that to grow. But I don't want you to hurt yourself. I want you to think smart. It's great to be spontaneous. I want that for you, too. But if your new thing is a huge leap that, if done wrong, will cause harm, then I want you to ask yourself a few questions:

"Am I ready for this?"

"Am I going to be able to enjoy it?"

"Am I going to be able to maintain it if necessary?"

Ask yourself these things before you begin your new thing. It's common to be afraid of doing something new. Please don't let that stop you. But also assess your risk. Think first, then leap.

Sometimes we are so desperate to have an experience that we don't think through what might come after. God said to me today, "I want you to be able to enjoy all your moments. I want you to be present in them. But I also want you to be prepared for them so that when the moment has passed, it still feels amazing."

And baby, Tab got it. I won't be caught out there next time. Whether it's on a mountain or in other areas of my life, I will do my homework and thoroughly prepare for each new adventure—so I don't leave it sick. How many of us have done something amazing, but weren't prepared for all that came with that thang, and at the end of it all we leave that experience spiritually, mentally, or even physically sick? We still might think it was worth doing. I know going snow-mobiling was definitely worth it. But I can do better next time. We should always *want* to do better.

TSA
(Tabitha Service Announcement)

The old saying goes "No pain, No gain."
While trying something new, we may experience
pain, but the gain will usually outweigh it!

From Tab's "New Thing" Catalog

Do a three-day detox. Sometimes we just need to eliminate things from our bodies and/or lives for a season. Whether it is a food or social media detox, try to spend some time without that thing that seems to have consumed you in order to restore, refresh, and reboot your body and soul.

Go to sleep and/or wake up earlier. Sleep is such an important part of a healthy life. Too many of us are used to not getting enough hours or rest and then we wonder why we're always exhausted. Honey, try going to bed just one hour earlier tonight or, if you can, try to wake up a little earlier to give yourself some room to ease into your day.

Start or end your day with a new affirmation. There's a gospel song that says "Sometimes you have to encourage yourself . . ." Ain't that it? I encourage you to come up with three or four affirmations that you can say to yourself when you wake up or go to bed. You'll be surprised how much your spirit will hear and respond to those words of kindness and care.

Do Something That Honors a Parent or Caregiver

"Honor your father and your mother,
that your days may be long."
—*Exodus 20:12 NKJV*

I did a new thing.

I did a photo shoot with my daddy.

Honey, this wasn't just selfies at the house. Tab shot a full-out Target campaign with my daddy, along with my stepmom and brother/best friend, Nick. I love my stepmom and Nick but baby, my heart was so full working with my daddy. All I kept saying today was "Oh my God! I got to work with my daddy! I got to work with my daddy!" To know that he would open their promotional magazine and walk into the Target store to see us right there next to each other, loving on each other, is a joy I can't even begin to describe.

It was truly a full-circle moment. When I was a little girl, my daddy had several jobs, and one was cleaning the post office. Sometimes my sister and I would tag along with him, helping him clean up. My job was to clean out the ashtrays, because back then, people smoked in their offices. I also had to take out the trash bags, clean the cans, and place new trash bags in the cans. Little Tab had no idea what was in store for her life more than thirty-five years later.

I had my dreams, of course. And they were big. I remember calling my daddy in 1997 from the fashion college I was attending in Miami, Florida, asking him to pick me up because I was going to quit to become an actress.

"Daddy, I've got to quit this school," I said. "I'm supposed to be acting, and one day when I'm famous, I'll pursue my fashion. I'll have a clothing line and my own designs. But for right now, Daddy, I'm not supposed to be at this school."

And he didn't fight me on it. He just said, "Okay baby, I'll be down there Saturday to pick you up."

So can you imagine what it felt like to call my daddy twenty-six years later and say, "Hey, Daddy, I'm going to have you flown to Miami for a photo shoot with me!" Honey, it was a true opportunity for me to tell him that his hard work, all the ways he has loved and supported and poured into me, has paid off. Today we were literally right down the street from where he picked me up back then. And I made good on my promise. I am now an actor with a successful fashion line at Target.

Look at God.

Another reason why my heart is so full is because my daddy is seventy-one years old, and I've become increasingly aware just how much every year counts. It should always count for all of us, but in my family dynamic, there is a pattern of people dying very young. My father is the oldest man still living in our family. He comes from a family where no man has lived past seventy. Because of this, he looks at summers like "I might only have a few summers left." So I thank God for this moment. I thank God that I get to celebrate this huge accomplishment with him. I can't wait for him to see his beautiful face on an endcap at his local Target. I know he will be amazed.

The hard truth is that we don't know how long we will have our elders with us—our parents, grandparents, godparents, aunts, uncles, and caregivers. And they have so much knowledge we can learn from. Too many times, younger folks think, *Oh, they don't know what they're talking about,* or *Things have changed.* But we can look at the state of our world now and see that certain things are exactly the same. Their wisdom is a blessing that can help us navigate that world.

Because many of our parents are on the later side of life, we have to be mindful to do things with and for them now, while they are still here. Because honey, I promise you will regret not doing it. When I first started dating and ultimately living with my husband, I was in my early twenties and madly in love. Before my mother got sick, she used to call or pop over to our house asking for me to go shopping with her. "Come ride with me, baby. Let's go shopping" or "Let's go to the mall for a few." And what did I say? "No, Moma. I want to hang out with Chance. We are going to do something." Do you know how much I wish I could go back and say yes? I said yes sometimes, but too often I said no. I would love to have that time back.

And that's it right there! We don't have as much time as we think we do. So when I think about sharing this time with my daddy, I realize that I'm simply giving back to him what he invested in me. Instead of him taking me school shopping or on a trip, I get to take him shopping or on a trip. In fact, I have the honor of doing him one better. I don't just take him shopping—I get to put him on the advertisement at the store where other people shop.

So I encourage you to make use of whatever time you might have left with your elders. Maybe you do something fun and creative, like actually taking your parents school shopping. Buy them a new bag with some books, journals, and pens; maybe even a brand-new outfit. Honey, I know they'd get a kick out of that!

Whatever you decide to do, know that you are creating new memories for them. You might be expanding their horizons in ways you can't even imagine. Baby, I took my seventy-one-year-old daddy on a vacation to an island in the Caribbean Sea. He stood on the beach for a good, long minute, looking at that crystal clear, blue water, and cried. I'm sure he never imagined he'd see such a thing.

Our elders are always thinking about time. They know that time is precious, and they have more years behind them than they do in front. So enjoy them.

And yes, I realize that there are people who don't have a loving relationship with a parent. Reading this chapter might have been hard for you. First, I love you. I understand. I also understand that you have the power to be what you never had. So maybe it's not a parent or grandparent for you. Maybe it's the elder who sits at the front desk on your job. Maybe it's your child's teacher that you do something nice for. However you imagine a loving mother or father to be, treat yourself that way first, and then give that love to someone else.

Here's the lesson from this extraordinary new thing I did today. *When we can, we must.* That's it. God kept telling me, "You're able to do these things, Tabitha, so make it happen." When Target was originally planning for this shoot, they wanted to cast models. I said, "Oh, no, honey! This one has got to be with my daddy. There's no other way to do it." And of course they have always been supportive and made it happen.

Listen, if we have the power to do something special for a parent or caregiver, then let's take the time to make it happen. Don't put it off. You never know how much that show of love will bless them. Maybe seeing my full-circle moment helped my daddy dream a little bit bigger for himself, even at seventy-one. Even my stepmom was happy. She said she felt like a model and kept saying, "I can't believe I'm going to be in a Target campaign." And my bestie/brother Nic was just oh so grateful. It did my heart so good to make them happy, and that's the power of sharing your new things with those you love. If you can, you must. Very good.

TSA
(Tabitha Service Announcement)

*If you can, then you should, but if you can't,
it's also okay. Don't beat yourself up about what
you can't do, embrace the things you can.*

From Tab's "New Thing" Catalog

Sit with your elders. Sometimes that's all they would love from us. To sit with them. To talk with them. Ask them about their dreams as a child. Ask them about their greatest memory and, if you can, try to recreate the moment for them. Let them take you down memory lane.

Take your elder on a fun date. Help your parents or caregivers or elder mentors get dressed up and then take them out on the town. They love good music? Take them to a jazz concert. They have a favorite author? Take them to that author's book signing.

Give them a photoshoot. This is one of my favorite things to do. If you are able, hire a makeup artist and hairstylist and really do it up for your elder. Get a photographer to shoot them like they're high-fashion models. Can't you see the big smile on granny's face now? And if your budget is limited, do their hair and makeup yourself (or ask a friend), and then shoot them with your phone. It will still show them how much you care to spend time with them.

Meet My Play Cousin . . .
Thomas Did a New Thing

My mother has supported me in ways I can't even begin to tell you. Growing up, she was a single mother raising me, my brother, and my younger sister in Philadelphia. She worked so hard but didn't always have the kind of money she would have liked to be able to take us here and there. And yet still, we had lots of love and faith to hold us down. She took us to church, taught us about God, and I'm so grateful for that. She also taught us to be good and loving people. So my new thing was that I decided to take my mother out on the ultimate date.

Listen, this woman was so surprised when I pulled up to her home in a rented Mercedes-Benz and told her that she was getting dressed and going out with me tonight.

"Boy, stop playing with me. What do you mean? I'm sitting here watching my show."

She's always at home watching her show. But not this night. I really wanted to give her the queen treatment.

I ran out of the house and to the car really quickly to get the dress I'd had an assistant at my job pick out for her. When I brought it into the house, her eyes lit up.

"What is this for?"

"I told you we're going out tonight."

"Oh my goodness," she said. I don't think I've ever seen my mother blush, but she did that day.

Thankfully, she stopped protesting. She surely put the dress on and off we went.

Like I said, we didn't have a lot of money growing up, but the one thing my mother would cook for us, especially on the days when she worked late, was spaghetti. We loved her spaghetti! So I thought it would be really amazing if I took her to the finest Italian restaurant in the city. When we pulled up to the restaurant, she just looked at me and said, "Boy, do you know how much this place costs?!"

"Don't you worry about how much it costs, Moma."

I had reservations so as soon as we went in, we were seated. We had a wonderful Italian dinner with all the fixings. Afterward, I'm sure she thought the night was over, but I was just beginning. I took her to one of her favorite places. Somewhere she used to take us when we were little to run out our energy, as she used to say. The waterfront! The lights on the Ben Franklin Bridge were blinking in beautiful neon colors. New Jersey was lit up across the Delaware River. And Moma just sat there looking at those lights, her eyes sparkling just as bright as they were.

A portion of the waterfront has now been turned into a roller-skating rink, and so after watching the black water lap against the boats that lined the shore, she sat on a bench with a custard and watched all the young people roller skate. When I looked over at her, I saw a tiny tear escape the corner of her eye.

She was so happy. And it felt so good to make her happy. Many times, when we do new things, we think that they have to be for ourselves. And of course, that's a good thing. We should do new things for ourselves. But this time, I thought it was important to do something for someone else. For someone who has given her all to me. Who has supported and loved me. In showing her a good time that night, my heart was filled with so much joy and love.

Find a Unique Way to Communicate with a Loved One

"We should seek out all the doors which still remain ajar, however slight the opening might be."

—Angela Y. Davis

I did a new thing.

I found a new way to communicate with my nephew, who is in prison.

He'd just turned eighteen when things went left. So very young. So impressionable. Running with the wrong crowd, he eventually, inevitably, found himself in the wrong place at the wrong time and doing the wrong thing. My nephew has spent thirteen years of his life in prison and has about eight more years to go. Maybe less. And every day I pray for him. I pray for his heart, his mind, and mostly that he keeps his spirit steady as he deals with all the things he sees while locked up.

For a long while, I would write him notes or send pictures, and he would often write me long letters. Before the COVID-19 pandemic, I would try to visit him when I could. It was great to be able to check in with him and make sure he was holding on and keeping his head up. Unfortunately, visits stopped due to COVID, and we had to rely on letters and occasional phone calls. He always expressed how great it was to send and receive letters in the mail. However, his letters had to go through so much processing. They had to be approved and processed before he could send or receive any mail, and all of that takes time. Recently, the prison implemented a new program that allows me to pay money into a system so we can text each other directly. The messages are fairly instant, with only a slight delay in transmission. It's so worth it to be able to communicate with him every day as opposed to waiting all week or longer for a letter. For those incarcerated most thoughts center on time. How much time he has left. What he can do with his time. What he can't do. So to be able to significantly cut back the time it takes to speak with a family member gives him something to look forward to.

That's why this week I thought I'd try something new.

Before, whenever we'd speak on the phone, it was so difficult to get my nephew to open up. It was mostly me asking "How are you feeling? What do you need?" and him giving very surface answers. I imagine he didn't want to burden me with stories of whatever he might have been experiencing. Yet I couldn't help but feel like there was more. More he wanted to say and maybe didn't know how. More I wanted to hear. He is my only nephew and we're only ten years apart, so in many ways he's like a little brother, and I grew up helping raise him. I love him so much, and because I've been feeling that desire to get to know him better, I recently began praying about how I can help him. I said, "God, how can I help him open up and have a deeper conversation with me? Yes, he's like a little brother, but I want to get to know the thirty-four-year-old man he's become." It didn't help that I haven't been able to see him because visitations were stopped by the pandemic. I needed to have another point of connection.

That's when I decided that I would send him a new word every day. I texted him: "Oh, I'm doing a new thing! I'm writing a new book, and I've decided I want to give you a word that we can share every day. I'll send a word and tell you what my intention for the word is. Then you can tell me your intention for it." Honey, when I tell you this truly changed our conversations?! It was like a fire was lit.

I'm so grateful for this word of the day. We have been going back and forth, and our conversations are so much richer and deeper. It's gotten to the point where, if for whatever reason, I don't send him the word before he wakes up, he'll text me and say, "Hey, Auntie, what's the word of the day?" He looks forward to it!

Don't we all need something to look forward to? Sometimes we go through things and we need something to hope for. Something to wake up for. It turns out that by doing something so seemingly simple for me, I was actually doing something big for him.

Today, the word was "control."

He said, "Man, I'm so glad you sent me this."

"Why?" I asked. "What's different about the word 'control' than all the other words?"

"Because I was just telling myself that I've got to get to a place where I can be okay with the things I can't control, and be mindful of the things I can. I have to work on that a lot."

Baby, do you know how my heart just soared when I read that?

And the funny thing is, I had the same thoughts about the word. I, too, have got to be okay with things I can't control and focus on what is in my power. We were on the same page, and that blessed me so much.

I truly believe that this new texting system is helping the incarcerated people in this prison mentally. It has certainly helped my nephew. He doesn't have the luxuries we have on the outside. He can't eat what he wants to eat, wear what he wants to wear, or go where he wants to go. And rightfully so. It's a prison. That's what happens when you serve time. But if we want to truly rehabilitate people, then we have to be more compassionate and consider their mental and emotional health in the same ways we would our own. Because honey, the truth is: there are some people who are not even incarcerated, but they are still living in a mental prison. They've convinced themselves that they can't eat what they want to eat, wear what they want to wear, go where they want to go, or live where they want to live. They've allowed the world to tell them what they can't do. And if we believe that connection and compassion can help those living in their own mental prison, why wouldn't it be the same for those who are in an actual physical one?

Words have so much power. The small gesture of sending my nephew a word a day is empowering him. It's giving him language and understanding that will serve him well when he's free. Since I've begun doing this, I've noticed a shift in the energy of his messages. Before, when we'd send each other letters, he'd write in ways that lined up with the gang affiliation he had before going in at eighteen. His letters and even some early texts were always strange to read, because he'd replace certain letters associated with a rival gang with his gang-approved ones. And on the one hand, I get it. I understand that he's in prison; he is just trying to survive. He's doing everything he can to make it home. But when he's talking to his auntie, I told him I wanted him to be free. He wasn't bound to any rules of the street. He didn't have to change himself in order to be approved by someone else. I want him to only and always be himself. And honey, guess what? His messages to me now are so different. He is vulnerable in his sharing. He is growing.

I'm so grateful to be able to take the time to do something so seemingly small that is clearly having a big impact. And I can't wait to have real conversations with him in person again so I can show him how the world has changed. Not only is this a new thing for me but hopefully these messages are setting future new and wonderful things for him. New leaves for him to turn over. New joys for him to have. New memories that we can both share together as family.

TSA
(Tabitha Service Announcement)

Only you should be in control of your mind.
If your actions are dependent on what other
people feel or think of you, then honey,
you are not free.

From Tab's "New Thing" Catalog

Leave a message. Take a few of those sticky notes and leave them in a special place for your partner or loved one. Imagine how loved they will feel when they see your words on the mirror or in their lunch bag.

Create a dance. Honey, I love to dance, and so do many of my family members. If your family is like mine, come up with a quick line dance that's unique to your loved ones. Maybe it's associated with a song that's a family favorite. Now, every time you get together with them, you'll be able to cut a rug and have a good time.

Play a song with a message. Sometimes we just don't have the words to truly express our love and appreciation for our loved ones. But maybe Stevie Wonder does. Or, honey, maybe Snoop Dogg. Whoever it is, send that song to your loved one or listen with them so they know exactly how you feel.

Do Something That Reveals Your Purpose

"I am here for a purpose."
—*Og Mandino*

I did a new thing.

If I'm honest, I've been struggling a bit to find the right words for this one. The words are wrapped in so much sorrow and grief but also in hope and peace. I initially thought that my new thing was going to be visiting two new cities. This time, Memphis and Nashville, Tennessee. I've been so excited for this trip because Tennessee is right beside my home state of North Carolina, but I'd only ever driven through it while driving coast to coast. I've never actually spent any time there, so it felt good to at least be geographically close to home.

I figured out pretty quickly, though, that Tennessee is very different from North Carolina. In both Memphis and Nashville, you can feel the musical influence. Blues and country and gospel are all very much in the air. There's a rhythm to those cities that I don't necessarily feel as much in North Carolina. And honey, I suspect it was that rhythm, that melody of hope in the middle of utter devastation, that held the state together today.

I was scheduled to speak tonight at Vanderbilt University, and as we were driving into Nashville from Memphis, we got the horrible news. Another mass shooting. A person with an AR-15 had walked into an elementary school and shot and killed six people, including three nine-year-old children. My heart broke, family.

Yes, I still had to speak. But as soon as I heard the news, I knew that this engagement would be different. I felt an intense sense of purpose wash over me as I prayed:

"God, there's no other reason for me to be scheduled to speak in Nashville on the night of such a tragedy except that you want to use me in a way I've never been used before. Give me strength. Give me guidance. Give me the right words. Make sure that I'm so present with these students even if my own sadness shows up."

It would have been so easy for me to allow myself to be overwhelmed with grief in this moment. However, I knew that somebody still had to show up for those who couldn't. Even in sorrow, somebody still had to be there. I also knew I was going to be surrounded by hundreds of students who needed some light, some joy, and I was willing to be that for them, even as I carried my own pain.

When I arrived at the hotel and then at Vanderbilt, I could

feel the sadness. It had blanketed the city. It's crazy how all the joy and excitement about coming to a city I'd never been to before just went away in an instant. I certainly was still happy to be there, but I now approached it as a purpose-driven mission. I wanted to make sure that I gave everyone I encountered love and compassion. Even if it was only a smile or a simple "Hello, how are you?" to a couple in the elevator. I know how much "It's going to be alright. Hang in there. It's been a tough day" means to someone I don't even know, standing in a hotel lobby. It can go a long way. Those small conversations are so big in these moments. They say "I see you. I feel you."

I took that same energy to Vanderbilt. The student board responsible for bringing me to campus met with me beforehand and said, "Thank you so much for coming today. We really need you. The students need light today." And I felt so blessed to be chosen for that moment that, honey, I went to the bathroom and prayed again. This time, my prayer was something totally different from what I'd normally pray before I speak. Tonight, my prayer was "God, let me be the light you intended for today."

Yes, I try to be a light all the time, wherever I go. But sometimes that light is different depending on the situation I'm walking into. People need to see something else when they are hurting. As soon as I finished praying and walked out of the bathroom, I felt a calming come over me. I can't even explain the kind of peace I felt. The moderator for the event, Claire, said she'd been crying all day but the sight of me calmed her spirit and restored her joy.

Yes! Use me, Lord.

Her words and the cosign from the audience were an answer to my prayer. I'm usually a light of joy and happiness. I'll always be that. But tonight I was a light of calm. Of peace. The storms in the hearts of these students were raging and they needed those waters stilled. They needed peace. And after the moderated conversation, I tried to pour my calm into every person I encountered in the auditorium. I gave hugs and took pictures and let each student know that it was okay to feel sad and to cry. It was also okay to be upset and want change! But in sadness and rage, I reminded them they had to stay focused. I shared that hatred wants to distract them from their own purpose, but they couldn't let that happen.

When I said "stay focused" to these students, I meant: don't let the world get too loud. This world can be noisy. And that noise can become a distraction if they aren't careful. Getting sucked into that noise might throw them off track and stop them from doing what they know they are supposed to do. Yes, stand up for what is right. Yes, make your voice heard. But also make sure that the hatred that feels so present sometimes doesn't override the love and joy you have inside. I guess when I say "stay focused" I am also saying, don't stop loving yourself. You can't spread love to others if you first don't have it within. Be kind to yourself. You need a break from the news? Take those apps off your phone. You need to cry? Go right on ahead and release it. I told each person tonight that it's okay to not be okay. They didn't need to be scared to talk to someone if they needed to.

Most college students I know have big dreams. I know I did. Knowing this, I wanted to encourage them to stay focused on that. Darkness is all around but it doesn't have to get inside us. And honey, I get that it's hard to fight when the world is so dark.

But it's also important that they/we focus on whatever light might be present. I shared with them that there is power in trying to see the good, the positivity in everything.

But most of all, I told them to keep going. Because isn't that what God wants of us? Even when things are hard. Even in a time of grieving. God wants us to trust Him enough to keep going. If we are grieving, then that means we are still here. Which means we still have work to do.

Can that be hard to digest? Honey, absolutely. Especially when we are grieving the loss of people, of babies. But as hard as that is, I truly believe that we're all placed here for our designated amount of time. We don't know the hour or day or how old we'll be when our time is up, but no matter what, we are sent here to make an impact. When children are taken, it's an unexplainable pain. But I also know that when children are taken, it shakes up the world. And we hope it will be a catalyst for change. A signpost for people to do better. My prayer is that everyone who came to see me tonight will stay focused on the good. Stay focused on the love. Stay focused on what God has placed inside of them to do. And if they all, if we all, can do that then the world absolutely can become a better place. We will all begin to heal together.

Tonight was a totally different Tabitha Brown event and I'm so grateful for that. Because it wasn't really a Tabitha Brown event at all. It was God showing up for those who were hurting.

Yes, when a tragedy happens, I show up online for those who have been hurt. I'll sometimes speak on the subject. But tonight, I got the privilege to do it one-on-one, in person. I felt blessed by that. I know God intended that. So yes, Nashville is certainly a music city. It's a city of rhythm. But tonight, the rhythm for me was purpose. It was a purpose-driven rhythm I was listening to. The people in that auditorium felt the rhythm of God, and hopefully that soothed their broken hearts for a little while. I pray that even as they fight, the people I spoke with tonight were, even if for just a moment, able to receive this offering and find their calm.

What does being a light of calm look like, especially in the face of someone who might be grieving? It might look like laughter. Or understanding. Or being a silent presence. That latter one trips us up sometimes. Honey, sometimes people don't need cheering up. I didn't walk into that auditorium to make people happy per se tonight. That wasn't the call today. Sometimes people just need to be able to process their sadness in a safe space. Being a light might just mean holding their hand, rubbing their back, letting them lay their head on your shoulder, all while you sit in silence. If they feel like laughing, of course laugh with them. But if you know that sitting beside them on the couch watching *The Golden Girls* will help give them some space in their minds for a bit, then do that, too.

One of my favorite ways to be a light for my loved ones is to share music with them. Music is so healing. We might dance or sing together. Or, again, we might just sit in silence and let the lyrics in a song wash over us. Just knowing that someone is there for us during our time of grieving is so comforting. Just knowing that if I happen to completely collapse out of sorrow there will be somebody there to catch me, to love me, to be patient with me and understand, well, that's what light does. And we all have the ability to be light for each other. And as the song says, "Lights will guide you home."

Keep following the light, family.

TSA
(Tabitha Service Announcement)

There are two definitions for the
noun form of light.
The natural agent that stimulates sight
and makes things visible.
An expression in someone's eyes indicating
a particular emotion or mood.
May you always use the power of your light to help
things be more visible. May you always be able to
exude a mood of light. You deserve that!

From Tab's "New Thing" Catalog

Speak life. Y'all know Tab loves some mirror talk. Take a minute and look into the mirror. Speak positive words to yourself, especially if you are feeling the weight of grief and rage.

Hug somebody. If you know that someone is struggling with personal or collective grief, see if they will allow you to hold them for a while. Physical touch is a powerful healer, and while some people aren't comfortable with that, there are many who long for it. Words are often not necessary. Just the love energy from a hug.

Share your joy. Today, be intentional about sharing whatever joy you might have. Smile at people you come across today. Make eye contact. Really listen when they speak. This can make people feel seen and loved.

Very Good

Honey, look at you. You did it! We did it! As we come to the end of our journey in trying new things, I want you to check in with yourself. How do you feel? Doesn't it feel good to check thirty things off your list right now? Or maybe you were just able to do ten. Or five. Well guess what? That's ten or five more new things under your belt than when you started. And let me add one more to your list. You've read a new book! See, even if you weren't able to do a single new thing in this book, you've still already started. Add "Reading Tab's book" to the list.

I'm super grateful to have gone on this journey with you and to have the privilege of sharing each new experience and what it taught me. Whether I felt a new feeling, conceived a new thought or idea, chose a new hairstyle, made a change in my relationships, picked up a new hobby—or an old one like the flute—I feel even more free within myself than before. Each time I do these challenges, I gain more insight and more trust in God's purpose for and presence in my life.

So let's talk through what you might take away from this experience. First, celebrate the fact that you did it. As I've said a few times on this journey, we don't do that enough. Stepping outside of your comfort zone and doing new things is a really big deal. Also, remember that taking on even the simplest new tasks—like trying a new fruit—can have a big impact on your mind and heart. Too many times, we think that doing something small doesn't have much of an effect on us, but it absolutely can. Take advancing the power of your yes, and maybe the power in your no, if that was a new thing for you. When we say yes to something new and no to old ways of thinking and being, honey, we can't help but to see change.

There is power in your yes and your no. They might seem like they're just words. But they aren't. They can have such a great impact on you if you let them. Saying yes to doing something new puts us on track to changing our lives and saying no means remaining the same.

I'm going to assume that you picked up this book because you were ready for change. Well, let's go! Take advantage of the power in your yes. The power in doing something new. We all deserve that. You deserve that.

My real hope is that you are encouraged to share with a friend, family member, or coworker some of these new things you do. Maybe that's how you can be light to someone else. So many times we learn that we can take our leaps of faith by seeing another person do it and come out better on the other side. Maybe you can be that person for someone you know or love. It doesn't have to be a full challenge of thirty consecutive days. It could just be you saying "You know what? I'm going to try something new today." and then inviting someone else to join you. Or honey, you can create your own challenge! Say to your friends in the group chat: "You know what, y'all? Let's do some new things together. Let's make it a family affair." Or in the workplace, try challenging your coworkers to do something new every day. Maybe they can take a different route to work or simply eat a different lunch. Then y'all can get together at the end of the week to talk it out. In this way, you're not only opening your own life to more joy, you are helping others do the same.

I make a habit of living outside of my baseline, my norm. I'm always trying something new. I like what it feels like when my life opens up because I've ventured out and did something different. I know that when I travel to a new place, have a new drink, or even just try a new lipstick, it changes me forever. My mind has been stretched to a new place. I feel more expansive, more free. And honey, I hope after finishing this book and challenge, you feel the same way, too. I want that for you.

I want this *I did a new thing* movement to travel all over the world. I want us all to come together to do new things. Without a doubt, it will bring us closer together. It will help us see each other better, love each other stronger, all while we are also loving and seeing ourselves, while we are discovering new things about ourselves. Because that's really what it's all about, right? When we open our minds to doing something new, we're also learning new things about ourselves. We are learning what we like and don't like. What we need to hold on to and what we need to release. We are learning how to treat ourselves well and take care of our minds, bodies, and spirits.

Don't you overdo it, though! Don't you dare say that Tab told you that you had to do something new every minute of every day. I know how some of us might be inclined to take this new thing too far, because we think we have to be perfect or we believe there is a right way to do this. I said this in the beginning and I'll say it again now: there isn't any right way to do this. Honey, if you don't do something new today, that's your business and it's okay. Give yourself some grace and try again when you can. Every day is a new day with new grace. Just stay focused on your intention. Make your intention to always be mindful and take care of you.

My entire goal for writing this book is to encourage you to live on the edge a bit, whatever that might look like for you. And then once you take your leap, bring someone else along with you. That's how we spread love. That's how we get free.

Like I said, I've been doing these new things for a long time. Go check out the hashtag on Instagram or Facebook titled #Ididanewthing. Honey, as I shared at the beginning of this book, I've been doing this challenge as far back as 2014. In fact, in those posts, you see the old Tab—before I was truly free—still out there doing new things. But I'm grateful for even the new things I did back then because it gave me a mindset that helps me now. It led to me feeling like I could do the ultimate new thing! To do something I never knew I could do: choosing me. I chose to be the me that God created me to be. I chose to be free.

I also chose to not worry anymore about what people thought of me. I chose to trust God with my entire life! That new thing changed my world, honey, and I realize now that I deserved this life all along. So, in closing, that's what I want for you. I want you to allow these new things you've done to lead to you doing the ultimate new things—choosing yourself. Choose freedom. Choose love. Because you deserve it, honey. You are so worthy.

Now, until next time, cousins. Y'all go about your *new* business. And have the most amazing day. But even if you can't have a good one, don't you dare go messing up nobody else's, ya' hear?

I see y'all in a new place soon, alright?

Very good.

'You Did a
New Thing!

Honey, now you know Tab wants you to do this challenge at your own pace. Whether you were able to do five new things or thirty—that's your business. However, I also want to make sure you have a place to write in all your new things so when you look back on this journey, you'll have a record of all that you've done. Use this space for exactly that, alright?

_____

_____

_____

_____

_____

_____

_____

_____

_____

_____

_____

_____

_____

You Did a New Thing!

_____

_____

_____

_____

_____

_____

_____

_____

_____

_____

_____

_____